# Shootouts, Killings, and War Heroes

## The History Hidden in Monument's Cemetery

# Shootouts, Killings, and War Heroes

## The History Hidden in Monument's Cemetery

Michael Weinfeld and John Howe

Filter Press, LLC

*Shootouts, Killings, and War Heroes: The History Hidden in Monument's Cemetery*
Copyright © 2024 by Michael Weinfeld and John Howe
First edition

Published by Filter Press, LLC

All rights reserved. Except for brief passages quoted in newspaper, magazine, radio or television reviews, podcasts, and electronic media, no part of this book may be reproduced in any form or by any means, electronic or mechanical, without permission in writing from the publisher.

Disclaimer: The authors have spent years researching Monument Cemetery. This book is the cumulation of that work. They apologize for any errors.

ISBN: (Paperback): 978-0-86541-264-4

Library of Congress Control Number: 2024945123

Cover design: Jordan Ellender
Cover photographs courtesy of the Michael Weinfeld Collection

Unless otherwise noted, all images courtesy of the Michael Weinfeld Collection

Filter Press, LLC
Westcliffe, Colorado
https://www.filterpressbooks.com/
719-481-2420

John dedicates this book to his sister, Anne Carleton,
for her constant encouragement.

Michael dedicates this book to his wife and
best friend, Tia M. Mayer.

Finally, to the many volunteers who have made
Monument Cemetery such a
beautiful and special place.

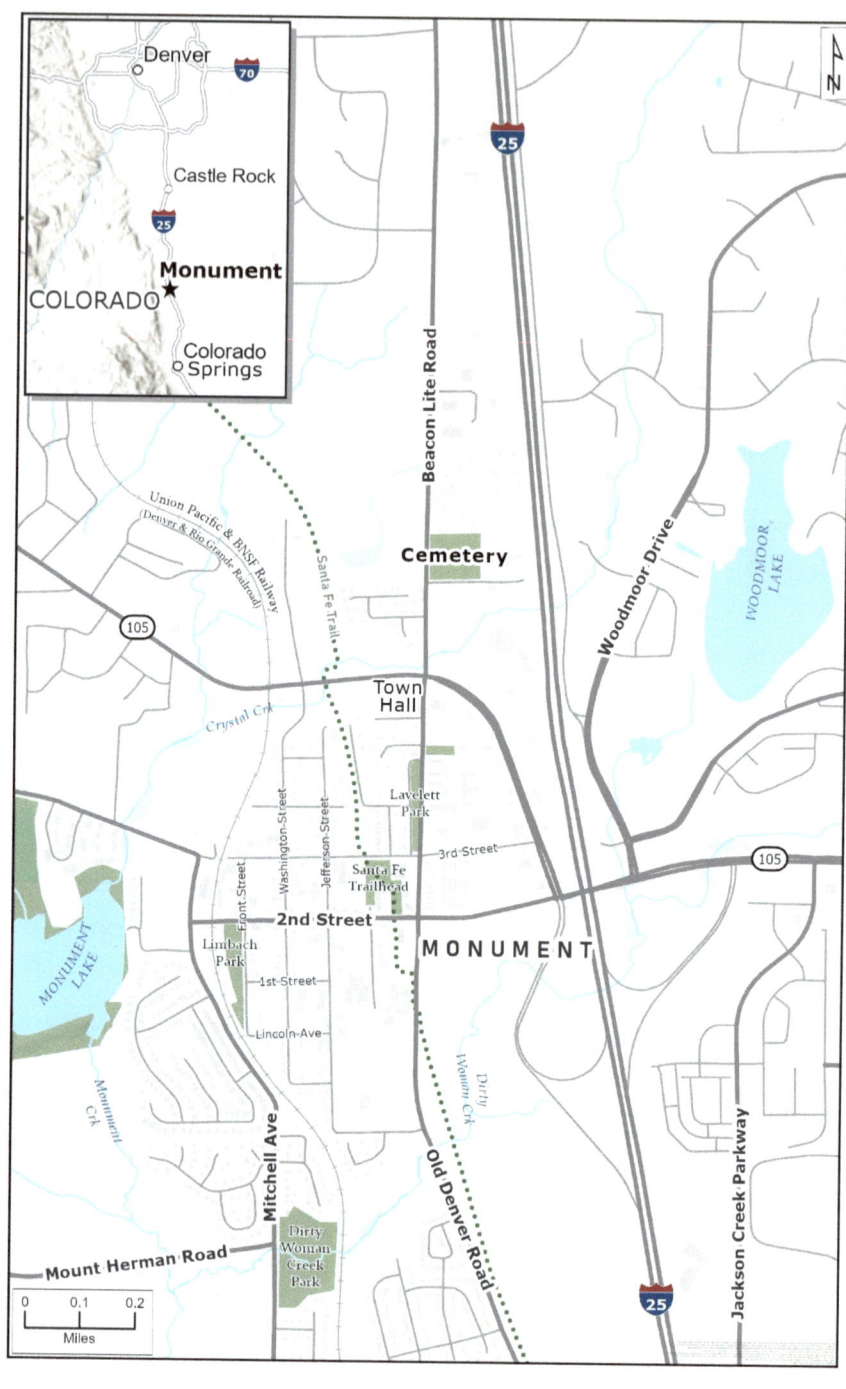

# Contents

Introduction ............................................................................. 1

CHAPTER 1: A Brief History of Monument ........................... 5

CHAPTER 2: Navigating the Cemetery ................................. 9

CHAPTER 3: Notable Graves ................................................ 12

    Francis M. Brown .............................................................. 12

    Henry and Caroline Limbach ........................................... 14

    Stephanie and Rachel Works ........................................... 16

    David and Catherine McShane ........................................ 18

    Isabella Trigg ..................................................................... 24

    Dr. William H. Rupp ......................................................... 26

    The Guires ......................................................................... 28

    John Olfs ............................................................................ 32

    Paton Wilson ..................................................................... 34

    Mary E. Doyle ................................................................... 36

    Charles D. Ford ................................................................. 39

    John W. and Emily Higby ................................................. 43

    Fred Simpson .................................................................... 47

    James Newbrough ............................................................ 50

    Moses F. Chandler ............................................................ 52

    Alonzo Welty ..................................................................... 54

CHAPTER 4: Memorial Day in Monument ........................... 55

**CHAPTER 5: Large and Unusually Shaped Gravestones** ............ 59

**CHAPTER 6: Cemetery Visits** ............................................................. 63

**CHAPTER 7: Who Is Right?** ................................................................ 66

**CHAPTER 8: Iron Fences** ................................................................... 73

**CHAPTER 9: Unusual Causes of Death** ............................................ 76

**CHAPTER 10: Other Interesting Discoveries and Information** ...................................................................................... 81

**CHAPTER 11: Cemetery Timeline with Significant Dates** ......... 85

Bibliography ........................................................................................ 119

Acknowledgements ............................................................................ 124

About the Authors .............................................................................. 125

Index ..................................................................................................... 126

# List of Figures

Figure 1: Folders containing information about Monument Cemetery ..................1
Figure 2: Three old handwritten ledgers identifying who was buried in the cemetery ..................2
Figure 3: An early hand-drawn map of cemetery and a more modern map of the cemetery ..................3
Figure 4: Monument Rock, the geological feature that gave the town of Monument its name ..................6
Figure 5: The 1892 Monument Potato Bake Festival ..................7
Figure 6: September 23, 1891, *Rocky Mountain News* picture ..................8
Figure 7: Welcome to the town of Monument ..................8
Figure 8: Views of Monument Cemetery ..................10
Figure 9: Monument Cemetery map showing blocks and sections ..................11
Figure 10: Gravestone of Francis M. Brown ..................13
Figure 11: Caroline Lindner Limbach and Henry Limbach ..................14
Figure 12: Gravestone of Caroline Limbach ..................16
Figure 13: Gravestones of Stephanie and Rachel Works ..................18
Figure 14: Catherine and David McShane ..................19
Figure 15: McShane Fort ..................20
Figure 16: Dedication of a historical marker placed near the site of the old McShane Stone Fort ..................21
Figure 17: McShane Fort plaque, 2024 ..................21
Figure 18: McShane Fort, 2024 ..................22
Figure 19: Monument Lake and its dam ..................23
Figure 20: Catherine and David McShane's headstone ..................23
Figure 21: Article in the November 3, 1904, *Elbert County Tribune* ..................24
Figure 22: Gravestone of Isabella Trigg ..................26
Figure 23: Gravestones of Dr. Rupp and his mother, Mary ..................27
Figure 24: Henry and Mary Guire ..................28
Figure 25: Grave markers of Mary and Henry Guire ..................30
Figure 26: Grave marker of David C. and Nancie Guire ..................31
Figure 27: The Olfs homestead ..................32
Figure 28: Gravestones of Harry Hagedorn and the Olfs ..................33

Figure 29: Potatoes grown in Monument, Colorado, circa 1908............ 34
Figure 30: Gravestone of Paton Wilson........................................................ 35
Figure 31: Doyle Ice & Storage Company, circa 1930............................... 36
Figure 32: Ice blocks loaded into train cars, circa 1920............................ 37
Figure 33: Cutting ice blocks from the Monument reservoir.................. 38
Figure 34: Mural celebrating Monument's ice harvesting history ........ 38
Figure 35: Gravestone of Mary Doyle.......................................................... 39
Figure 36: Advertisement from the August 16, 1882, *Castle Rock Journal* for the Monument Hotel .......................................................... 40
Figure 37: Monument Hotel .......................................................................... 40
Figure 38: Colonel Francis R. Ford and his wife, Henrietta.................... 41
Figure 39: Ford Family headstones .............................................................. 42
Figure 40: Mr. and Mrs. J. W. Higby ............................................................ 43
Figure 41: The Higby dry goods store in Monument ............................... 44
Figure 42: The Chapala Building which currently houses Covered Treasures bookstore ....................................................................... 45
Figure 43: Safe that originally belonged to the Higby Mercantile Company.............................................................................................. 45
Figure 44: Historical plaque on the Chapala Building honoring the Higby family ....................................................................................... 46
Figure 45: Gravestones of John and Emily Higby..................................... 46
Figure 46: Fred Simpson with his dog Rover and the mountain lion Simpson killed................................................................................... 47
Figure 47: October 28, 1922, *Denver Post* reporting of Simpson's killing of Old Disappearance............................................................. 48
Figure 48: Old Disappearance in the Lucretia Vaile Museum in Palmer Lake, Colorado .............................................................................. 49
Figure 49: Grave markers of Fred Simpson and his wives ..................... 49
Figure 50: Private James Newbrough ......................................................... 50
Figure 51: Headstone of James W. Newbrough......................................... 52
Figure 52: Chandler's advertisement of his blacksmith business ......... 52
Figure 53: Gravestone of Moses and Alice Chandler .............................. 53
Figure 54: Alonzo Welty's gravestone ......................................................... 54
Figure 55: Gravestone of Civil War veteran A. B. Simpson .................... 55
Figure 56: Marker of World War I veteran Benjamin C. Marston......... 56

Figure 57: Headstone of Glenn F. Melton, US Army, World War II .....56
Figure 58: Memorial Day, May 29, 2023.................................................57
Figure 59: Memorial Day, May 29, 2023, with Palmer Ridge High School graduate Michael Carlson playing taps ........................................57
Figure 60: Gravestones of veterans William J. Austen and William T. Crenshaw..................................................................................58
Figure 61: Grave and information about vetran Francis M. Agnew .....58
Figure 62: Marker of slain siblings Ryan Charles Willhite and Scarlett Christine Gallagher ...................................................................59
Figure 63: The Tucker family headstone.................................................60
Figure 64: Marker of Hiram Martin "Randy" Chamberlain...................60
Figure 65: Headstone of Carol M. and K. Charles H. Kleeberg............61
Figure 66: Headstones of Sylvia Gorball and Jennie Bishop .................61
Figure 67: Gravestone of Joshua Singh and the Ducommun family.....62
Figure 68: Authors Howe and Weinfeld poking around Monument Cemetery ...............................................................................64
Figure 69: Emblems of the Hassell and Stewart Iron Works .................73
Figure 70: Monument Cemetery fence built by the Hassell Iron Works Company ....................................................................74
Figure 71: Prison cells at Alcatraz Federal Penitentiary .......................74
Figure 72: Monument Cemetery fence built by the Stewart Iron Works Company....................................................................75
Figure 73: Ironwork from the Stewart Iron Works Company ................75
Figure 74: Death certificate of Vergal Bishop ........................................76
Figure 75: Death certificate of Everett Eckerson ...................................77
Figure 76: Gravestones of Everett Eckerson and his three children......78
Figure 77: Death certificate of T. J. Chase .............................................78
Figure 78: Gravestone of Thomas J. Chase.............................................79
Figure 79: Gravestone of Fred Krueger ..................................................83
Figure 80: John Howe at our work table ................................................84
Figure 81: Quit claim deed for Monument Cemetery .............................86
Figure 82: R. H. Ashworth's platting of Monument Cemetery...............88
Figure 83: 1909 train wreck near the town of Husted.............................89
Figure 84: Headline and story on the front page of the August 16, 1909, *Durango Semi-Weekly Herald*........................................90

Figure 85: Gravestone of Bertha Curry ........................................................ 91
Figure 86: The store of J.M. Brown, formerly owned by Will Lierd ..... 92
Figure 87: A robbery at the store of J. F. Roth .......................................... 92
Figure 88: Headstone of James Simpson ..................................................... 93
Figure 89: Certificate of death for James Blaine Simpson ..................... 93
Figure 90: Gravestone of John Bougher ...................................................... 95
Figure 91: Lucille Lavelete standing with two Monument Cemetery Association members ................................................................. 96
Figure 92: Historian Lucille Lavelett ........................................................... 97
Figure 93: Article about the July 9 cemetery vandalism ........................ 99
Figure 94: Article describing the controversy of the cemetery beautification project ..................................................................................... 100
Figure 95: Crematory Garden, 2024 ........................................................... 106
Figure 96: Worker using ground-penetrating radar and a resulting scan ................................................................................................... 114
Figure 97: Plaster marker used to mark the remains found with ground penetrating radar ..................................................................... 114
Figure 98: A new "unknown" granite headstone and Kent Griffith in front of a new headstone ............................................... 117
Figure 99: John Howe's marble bench and the presentation of Howe's bench in October 2017 ................................................................. 118

# Introduction

It started with a conversation in July 2010, when John Howe was helping the Monument town gardener, Sharon Williams, hand-water plants in the town cemetery. Williams mentioned in passing that Monument was looking for someone to update the cemetery records. Howe thought that sounded interesting, so he volunteered.

The town estimated that the project would be completed by the end of the year. Howe went to work in the town hall, assembling the various sources of information. There were nine drawers full of file folders describing most of the people buried in the cemetery, but some files were missing.

Figure 1: Folders containing information about Monument Cemetery. The folders were filled with handwritten and typewritten pages. Some of the information was written on scraps of paper.

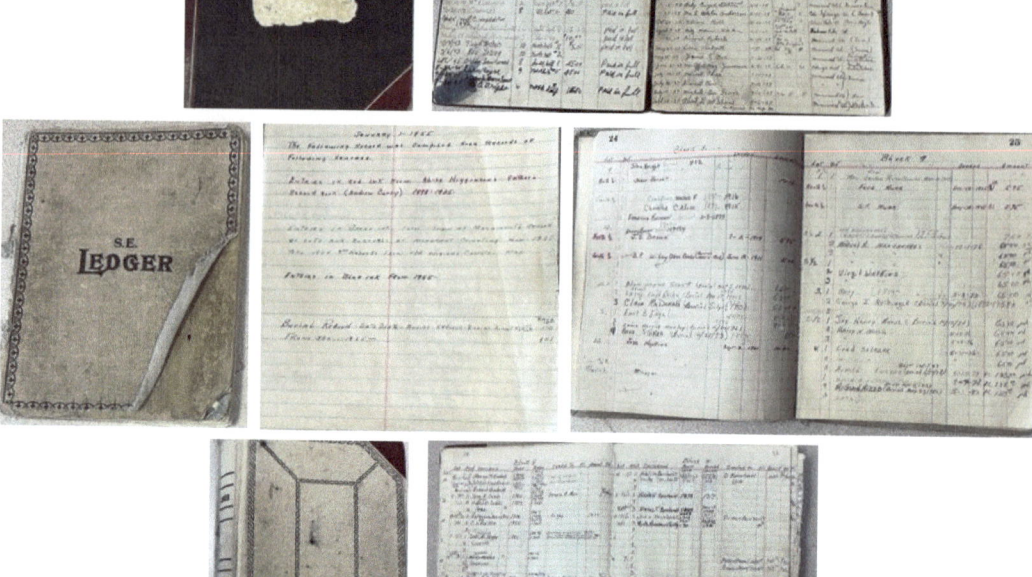

**Figure 2:** Three old handwritten ledgers identifying who was buried in the cemetery. The ledgers often had loose pages, like the one shown in the center.

There were also three old handwritten ledgers identifying burial sites, but occasionally the information in the ledgers didn't match other records. Though the transcribers had done their best to copy the facts from one source to another, they had made mistakes or had not verified the information. Also, their handwriting could be difficult to read.

# Shootouts, Killings, and War Heroes

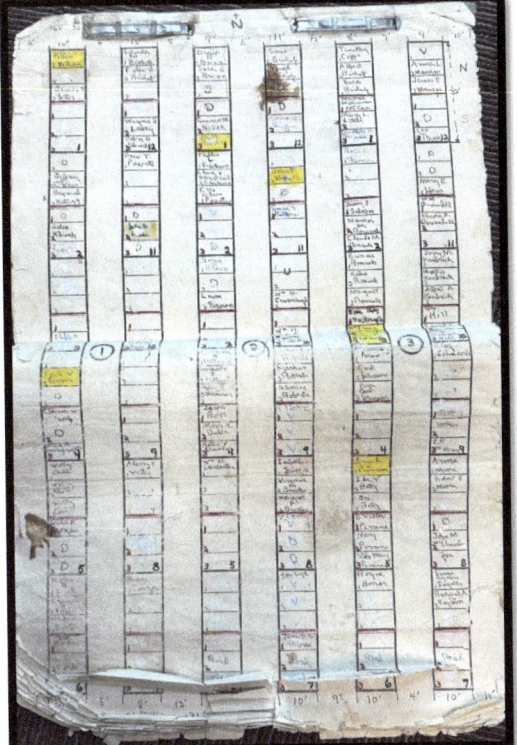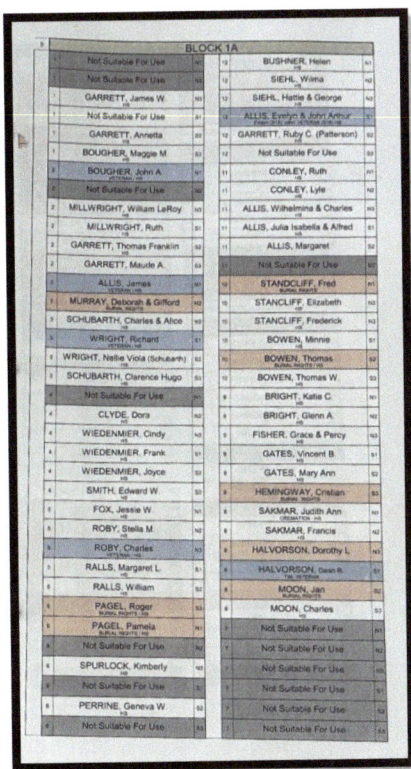

Figure 3: An early hand-drawn map of the cemetery (left) and a more modern map of the cemetery (right).

There were also several crudely drawn maps of the cemetery. At first, the entries were written in pencil, then ink; eventually they were typewritten. Sometimes the information was copied incorrectly.

There was also a map created by ground-penetrating radar.

Howe made notes of what had to be followed up on or cross-checked. One source he used for cross-checking was a book compiled by the town's cemetery sexton, *Tombstone Inscriptions of the Monument, Colorado Cemetery*, published by the Pikes Peak Genealogical Society. Unfortunately, the information in this book didn't always match other sources.

It soon became obvious that the project would last much longer than the expected six months. In fact, it ended up taking fourteen years!

In the summer of 2018, a few months after moving to Monument from Herndon, Virginia, Michael Weinfeld joined Howe. The two had met while doing interviews for Monument's 140th anniversary celebration. Howe mentioned his cemetery project and Weinfeld volunteered to help. Weinfeld and his wife, Tia M. Mayer, had always been interested in cemeteries. Howe said Weinfeld's assistance immediately proved invaluable. His curiosity and online investigative techniques helped correct or add to the more than sixteen-hundred files.

This book is the product of our thousands of hours of research and countless visits to the cemetery. We hope you enjoy the history and stories we discovered as much as we have.

*Michael Weinfeld and John Howe*

**CHAPTER 1**

# A Brief History of Monument

According to the Palmer Lake Historical Society, the Kiowa, Mountain Ute, Cheyenne and Arapahoe Tribes passed through the area where the town of Monument is now located. Among the first European settlers were Henry Guire and his family, who traveled by wagon train across the plains in the summer of 1864. *The Colorado Springs Gazette-Telegraph* reported on August 28, 1960, that the Guires arrived in the spring of 1865 after spending time in Golden. They set up a homestead near the home of David McShane and his wife Catherine, who lived on a 160-acre settlement.

Although most pioneers probably arrived by covered wagon, some traveled by stagecoach. Monument resident Sharon Williams learned from several descendants of pioneers that there was a stagecoach stop at a house on the corner of Second Street and Jefferson Street, where Lolley's Ice Cream presently operates. Williams said that the house

Figure 4: Monument Rock, the geological feature that gave the town of Monument its name

behind Lolley's served as an infirmary, where sick travelers could be treated.

In 1871, the Denver & Rio Grande Railroad built a line between Denver and Colorado Springs, with a stop near what would later become the town of Monument. The stop was located on Henry Limbach's ranch, so the town was initially called Henry's Station.

Initially the town was mostly a farming and ranching community. When supplies started arriving by train, settlers created businesses. On June 2, 1879, the town was incorporated; Limbach became the first mayor. In 1874, the town's name was changed from Henry's Station to Monument Station, named after a tall white rock formation to the west, and then in 1882 it was shortened to Monument.

In the late 1800s, Monument was known for the potatoes grown in the surrounding area. An article in the September 23, 1891, *Rocky Mountain News* described the Divide Potato Bake and Barbecue Association was organized in the autumn of 1889. After two unsuccessful attempts, Monument celebrated its first Potato Bake Festival on September 22, 1891.

Figure 5: The 1892 Monument Potato Bake Festival with the Denver & Rio Grande train station on the right and the Park Hotel on the left
*Courtesy of the Palmer Lake Historical Society*

The newspaper headline stated, "IT WAS A SUCCESS" and described the event in glowing terms:

> The tables, figuratively speaking, were fairly groaning under the weight of beef, pork, mutton, potatoes, bread, pickles, coffee and all other necessaries, together with not a few luxuries. The whole crowd ate—ate to the full—and still there remained tons of excellent food, with no one to partake thereof. Everybody praised the dinner as they thanked the generous hosts for their superb hospitality.

The newspaper went on to report that residents and dignitaries from all over the state, including Colorado governor John Routt and his wife, Eliza, came to Monument to eat potatoes, watch a parade, and play games. Prizes were awarded

Figure 6: The September 23, 1891, *Rocky Mountain News* included this picture with its Potato Bake Festival article.

to the best potato dishes and the Denver & Rio Grande Railroad offered special rates to those traveling to the event.

Local historian Linda Case states that blight caused by insects common on wild rose bushes crippled the potato industry. The festival ended in 1917.

According to the 1920 census, there were fewer than two hundred people living in Monument then. In comparison, the 2020 census reported more than ten thousand people living in and around the town. The town continues to grow rapidly (some would say too rapidly).

Monument is now part of the Tri-Lakes area, made up of Monument, Palmer Lake and Woodmoor. It is home to many artists and is known statewide for its Fourth of July parade.

Figure 7: Welcome to the town of Monument

**CHAPTER 2**

# Navigating the Cemetery

Monument Cemetery is located at 800 Beacon Lite Road, one mile north of the Monument town center. It covers a little more than five acres, most of which were donated by Charles Bissell in 1886, and currently has 1,692 burial plots. Monument pioneers, victims of the 1918–1919 influenza epidemic, and some of those who died in a local train crash are buried there. It is open from 8:00 a.m. to sunset and visitors are always welcome.

When searching for an individual interred in the cemetery, knowing the grave's location (or plot) makes it easier to find, although some location signs in the cemetery can be confusing. The cemetery is divided into twenty-two blocks, and each block has two rows running north and south. The blocks are split into sections. The first six sections are on the west side of the cemetery, and Sections 7-12 are on the east side. Each section is divided into six plots, and each plot can accommodate one full-size burial and two cremations, or four cremations.

Figure 8: Views of Monument Cemetery

Facing north

Facing west

Facing east

Facing south

There is also a crematory garden and each plot in this garden can hold a single cremation. An example of a grave location would be Block 1, Section 8 N1, with the *N* standing for "north" (and *S* standing for "south").

As of this writing, the cemetery is sold out.

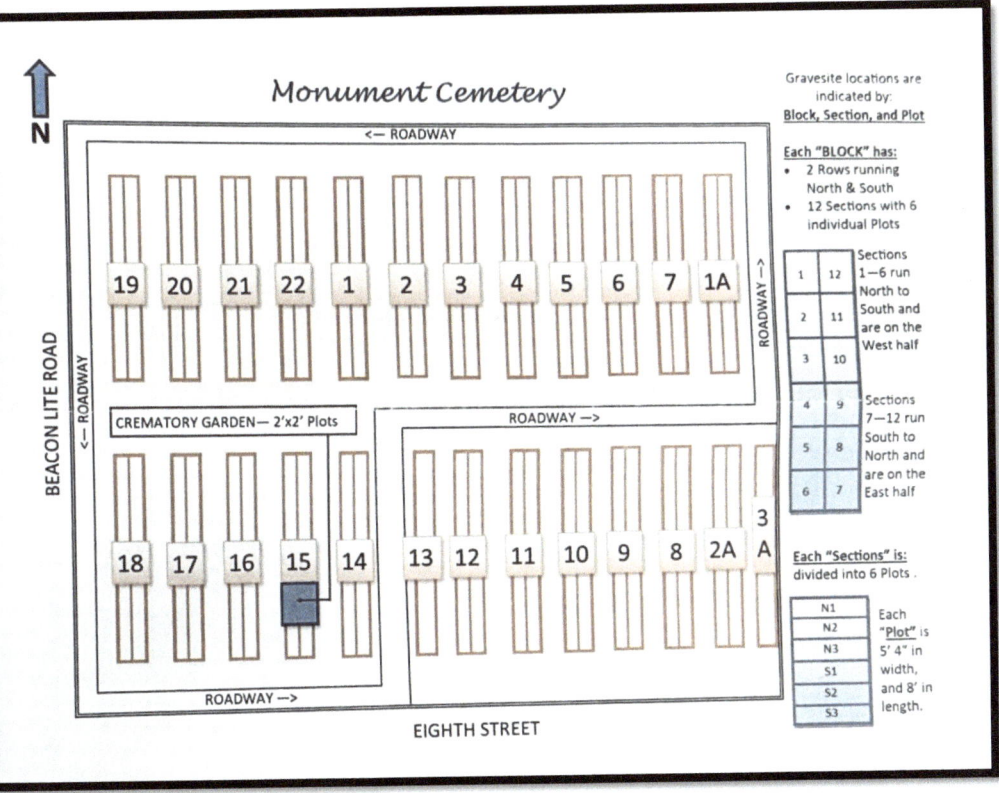

Figure 9: Monument Cemetery map showing blocks and sections

**CHAPTER 3**

# Notable Graves

There are numerous notable graves with fascinating stories behind each individual and their death. The following are a few of the more interesting histories hidden in Monument Cemetery.

**Francis M. Brown**
**What Would an Old West Town be Without a Shootout?**

It was a Saturday afternoon, October 21, 1876, around five o'clock, when a pioneer named Francis M. Brown, also known as Major Brown, got into an argument with a pioneer named Daniel Davidson in Henry Limbach's grocery store. According to the October 25, 1876, *Colorado Mountaineer*,

Figure 10: Gravestone of Francis M. Brown, Block 18 Section 9 S1

eyewitnesses testified before the coroner's jury that Brown accused Davidson of stealing cattle from a Mr. Rule. One eyewitness, David McShane, stated that Davidson said, "Any man who said that he stole old man Rule's cattle was a damned liar." Davidson then shot Brown twice and killed him.

Brown was thirty-seven years old and his gravestone says simply, "Who was killed."

Davidson was put on trial in 1877. *The Colorado Springs Gazette* reported on February 17 that when the murder indictment was read in court, Davidson "fainted and fell to the floor. He was restored to consciousness by water dashed in his face." After he was seen by a doctor, Davidson was taken to jail.

In March, Davidson was found guilty of manslaughter in the first degree. He was sentenced to five years hard labor in the Colorado State Penitentiary in Cañon City. Lucille Lavelett wrote in her book, *Through the Years at Monument, Colorado*, that Davidson's attorney fought the verdict. In May

1877, Davidson was released upon giving a bond of $5,000.

For three years, Davidson's attorney sought a new trial, eventually winning one in February 1880. *The Rocky Mountain News* reported on February 13, 1880, that Davidson's attorney convinced the jury the shooting was self-defense. Davidson was found not guilty. Lavelett wrote that in 1881, Davidson was elected to a Monument town board. As a board member, Davidson helped pass an ordinance prohibiting the shooting of firearms in town.

## Henry and Caroline Limbach
### German immigrants who made their mark in Monument

Henry Limbach arrived in the United States in 1863. He enlisted at Tarrytown in the Forty-First New York Volunteer Infantry during the Civil War, serving in Company C. In 1864, he transferred to Company B, mustering out in 1865. He came

Figure 11: Caroline Lindner Limbach and Henry Limbach
*Courtesy of the Palmer Lake Historical Society*

to the West in 1866 as a captain in the Eighth Cavalry.

He and Caroline Lindner had been schoolmates in Germany. In her book about Monument, Lavelett states that Caroline came to America with her mother, Maria, in 1872. It was arranged that Henry and Caroline would marry in St. Louis in May of that year.

Once they were married, Henry took his bride to his ranch at Henry's Station (later Monument Station), a whistlestop on the Denver & Rio Grande Railroad.

Caroline did not speak English when she arrived. She was the first known White woman to settle in the Monument area. Lavelett wrote that when their son Ed was born, a Caucasian baby was such an oddity that friendly Native Americans would stop by to gawk at him.

The town of Monument was incorporated on June 2, 1879, and Henry Limbach became the first mayor, serving from 1880 to 1882. He was also the postmaster from 1871 to 1881.

In 1883, Charles Adams donated land bordered by Second Street and Front Street for use as a park. It was named after Limbach because he planted the trees and seeded the grass there in 1884. Today that park is used for picnics, Wednesday night concerts, and daylong musical performances on the Fourth of July. At first, the Fourth of July concerts were held on the back of a wagon owned by one-time mayor Si Sibell, whose horse Baron could often be seen wandering through town. In 2007, the current bandstand was built along with a playground and restrooms. Limbach lived at 221 Front Street and as of 2024, his house was still there.

Caroline Limbach ran a dry goods, millinery, and dress shop at the corner of Front and Second Streets for twelve years. She died in 1894 and is buried in Monument Cemetery next to her mother.

Figure 12: Gravestone of Caroline Limbach,
Block 7 Section 12 N1

Henry Limbach is not buried in the town he founded. He outlived his wife by twenty-four years. He moved to Denver in 1909 and is buried in Fairmont Cemetery.

## Stephanie and Rachel Works
### Teenagers Killed outside the New Life Church

Teenagers Stephanie and Rachel Works were in the family minivan with their parents when twenty-four-year-old Matthew Murray started shooting outside the New Life Church in Colorado Springs on December 9, 2007. Stephanie, age eighteen, Rachel, age sixteen, and their father, David Works, were hit. Stephanie died at the scene and Rachel later succumbed to her wounds at Penrose Hospital.

According to the May 6, 2016, *Denver Post*, David Works said, "I was just fastening the seat belt and I heard a loud bang. I looked around and I saw this guy in black. He started shooting us up."

After shooting the girls and their father, the gunman went inside the church where he started "spraying gunfire into doors and the hallway and causing congregants to scramble into rest rooms, under desks and under the stage in the sanctuary for cover," according to a 460-page Colorado Springs police report.

A volunteer security guard named Jeanne Assam confronted the shooter. Assam, a forty-two-year-old former police officer, had been with the church for only a few months. She told a news conference after the shooting, "I took cover. I identified myself. I engaged him." She fired five shots, wounding the gunman.

Police sergeant Skip Arms told the *Associated Press* that after Assam injured the gunman, he killed himself with a shot to the head. Newspapers also reported that about twelve hours earlier, the gunman had shot and killed two people and wounded two others at the Youth With a Mission training center in Arvada, Colorado, eighty miles away. The dead were identified as Tiffany Johnson, age twenty-six, and Philip Crouse, age twenty-four.

Stephanie and Rachel Works had spent their summers and vacations on missionary trips in nations around the world, including India. The big wheel located near Stephanie and Rachel's graves was donated by India in the girls' memory.

The May 6, 2016, *Denver Post* wrote that the girl's father said, "Not a day goes by that you don't miss your daughters—

Figure 13: Gravestones of Stephanie and Rachel Works behind a wheel India donated in their memory, Block 9 Section 5 S1 and S2

it is with me all the time."

## David and Catherine McShane
## The McShane Fort

David and Catherine McShane settled on a 160-acre homestead in Monument in the spring of 1865. On September 22, 1868, *The Rocky Mountain News* reported on a Native American raid near Monument Creek. A house was burned and fifteen to twenty head of stock were taken. The article

**Figure 14: Catherine and David McShane**
*Courtesy of the Palmer Lake Historical Society*

states:

> Several Indians came into the house of Mr. McShane, where there were several women alone and a horse picketed near the door. As an Indian was about to take the horse Mrs. McShane said to him, "Don't take the horse;" the Indian replied, "No take horse—take scalp!" "Very well," said Mrs. McShane; "take the horse." The Indian took the horse and said, "Thank you, mam."

To keep his family safe from another attack, David McShane built a stone fort with an underground passage to his house. The fort was used from 1865 to 1868. The September 7, 1902 *Rocky Mountain News* reported on the original fort, which was rebuilt that year:

> The fort was built about six feet above ground and the floor three feet below the surface. The walls were made thick and the top covered with timber and then with earth. Five or six rifle holes were made through which they could

**Figure 15: McShane Fort**
*Courtesy of the Palmer Lake Historical Society*

shoot and close them at will. An underground passage led from the house through which the family, when alarmed, could go without danger into the fort. . . .

During the Indian uprising of 1868 the old fort protected forty-six children that belonged to nine families.

Lavelett described the fort in *Through the Years at Monument, Colorado*. She wrote that the doors were narrow, and four portholes could be closed with sliding stone blocks. A fifth porthole was used to watch for Indians. The roof was made of logs covered with earth so that Indians couldn't set it on fire. In her *Tri-Lakes Tribune* column "Monument Happenings and Histories," local historian Linda Case reported that someone would ride daily to a hill called the Lookout to watch for Native Americans. If they spotted any, they'd tell everyone to get in the fort.

Figure 16: Dedication of a historical marker placed near the site of the old McShane stone fort, as shown in the February 25, 1971, *Palmer Lake-Monument News*

Figure 17: The McShane Fort plaque, 2024

A total of sixteen families used the fort at one time or another. They're listed on a plaque on Highway 105 in Monument near Palmer Lake. The plaque is west of the railroad bridge and 610 feet south of the fort's location. The family names on the plaque are Guire, Brown, Jackson, Shideler, Chandler, McShane, Teachout, Davidson, Oldham, Walker, DeMasters, Roberts, Watkins, Faulkner, Simpson, and Welty.

**Figure 18: McShane Fort in 2024**

Dignitaries from the Zebulon Pike and Kinnikinnik chapters of the Daughters of the American Revolution (DAR) presented the marker to the state of Colorado in 1950. The dedication ceremony was attended by former lieutenant governor William E. Higby; DAR historian Dorothy Buren; state historian LeRoy Hafen; Mrs. Roy Davis, regent of the Zebulon Pike chapter of the DAR; and Mrs. John Crouch, vice regent of the Kinnikinnik chapter.

Descendants of the McShanes also attended the dedication. *The Palmer Lake-Monument News* reported that the crowd heard "vivid accounts of old killings and scalpings" and how Catherine McShane and other brave pioneer women protected their children and homes while the men were away working.

The 1902 *Rocky Mountain News* article reported that David and Catherine's son Albert restored the fort to its original height. The fort had partially crumbled, and pieces had been carried back east as relics.

David McShane helped build three schoolhouses in Monument, including the town's first schoolhouse. He and General Charles Adams donated the land where Monument Lake (originally the state reservoir) was built in 1892, and he helped build the dam there. The August 29, 1892, *Rocky*

Figure 19: Monument Lake (left), and the dam of Monument Lake (right)

*Mountain News* reported that the reservoir covered seventy-two acres of land. According to the town of Monument website, today Monument Lake is less than half that size, only 30.7 acres. Monument Public Works Facilities Superintendent Ron Rathburn says that by the 1970s, the forty-two-foot-tall dam had crumbled badly. The lake had to be drained so that the dam could be rebuilt. In the process, the lake was made smaller. When the body of water was first created, it contained 400 million gallons of water. Today's lake contains only about 100 million gallons.

McShane was also Monument's first postmaster, and the first post office was on his ranch. He was also a delegate to various territorial and state conventions and in 1869, he was elected county commissioner. McShane died in 1907, nine years after, Catherine.

Figure 20: Catherine and David McShane's headstone with the Freemason's symbol at the top, Block 16 Section 1 N2 and N3

## Isabella Trigg
## A Brave and Fearless Woman

According to her obituary, Isabella Trigg settled in Monument in 1866. She had two children, but it is unknown what happened to her husband; he is not mentioned in her obituary. Isabella Trigg filed for three land patents on December 16, 1871, and the United States issued land assessments in her name alone. She individually continued to acquire land in the Monument area, making a living as a farmer. On January 30, 1878, *The Rocky Mountain News* reported that she had sold hay to John Chestnut, who paid $250 with a forged check.

Figure 21: Article in the November 3, 1904, *Elbert County Tribune*

Her obituary, published on the front page of the November 3, 1904, *Elbert County Tribune*, tells the story of the most exciting day in her life.

Trigg is described in the obituary as "one of her [Colorado's] oldest and best known pioneers, as well as one of the bravest and most fearless women whose name is closely connected with the early history of the state." The article reads as follows:

Mrs. Trigg had been a

resident of Monument since April 3, 1866, and was a member of the little band of men and women who in 1868 defended themselves for several weeks from the hordes of Indians, at the McShane house, where they had built a fort. Among the brave defenders were Mr. and Mrs. Jacob Guire and their pretty golden-haired and blue-eyed little son, Andrew Jackson Guire. During an apparent cessation in hostilities, during which the redskin hordes had seemingly abandoned the siege of the fort and withdrawn, the boy asked permission to go into the back yard of the ranch and play.

Permission was granted and the lad stepped outside. He had been outside but a few minutes when suddenly and without warning a war-painted Indian mounted on a swift pony darted over a knoll a short distance away and rode straight toward the spot where little Andrew was playing on the ground. The Indian's right arm was lifted and in his hand he grasped a shining tomahawk. It was his intention to slay the little paleface.

But the redskin was not quick enough to accomplish his sanguinary deed, for Mrs. Trigg, who had been looking out of the window, saw him coming. She threw her own little boy and girl, who were with her, on the bed and covered them up with a blanket. Then she jumped through the open door, seized the boy and literally hurled him into the kitchen just as the Indian swooped by the door. The redskin, seeing his prey escape, turned his pony and darted after the brave woman with the blood curdling cry, "Heap big black hair," meaning the long tresses of Mrs. Trigg would make a fine scalp.

Again the brave white woman defeated the redskin's purpose. She sprung through the kitchen door and slammed it shut just in time to escape being struck with the tomahawk which the Indian hurled at her and imbedded itself in the heavy oak timbers of the door.

Her obituary states that Trigg died on October 19, 1904. It should be noted that her gravestone says "Isabell Triggs" instead of "Isabella Trigg," the spelling found in all other documentation. The cemetery ledgers and maps list her as "Isabelle Triggs."

Figure 22: Gravestone of Isabella Trigg, incorrectly marked as "Isabell Triggs,"
Block 2 Section 8 N1

## Dr. William H. Rupp
## A Doctor Who Never Billed his Patients

William H. Rupp was an old-fashioned country doctor who looked the part. Marion Savage Sabin wrote in her 1957 book, *Palmer Lake: A Historical Narrative*, that Rupp "wore a mustache, was dressed in a frock coat and a broad, black felt hat and always carried the traditional black bag." She further described him as a "tall, spare figure," a gray-haired man in his fifties or sixties.

According to Lucille Lavelett, Rupp came to Monument from Illinois to get help for his asthma. His first office was on Front Street and later he bought the Monument Hotel and moved his office there. Lavelett wrote that Rupp never sent a bill to his patients. He figured if they could afford to pay, they would. Rupp never owned a car. Sabin wrote that Rupp got around town in a top buggy behind a team of bays. He was also the town treasurer and water commissioner.

The November 20, 1920, *Colorado Springs Gazette* reported that Rupp's mother, Mary K. Rupp, died at her son's home on the morning of November 19, 1920. She was ninety-four years old. Her son is buried next to her.

The Sunday *Gazette & Telegraph* reported on August 23, 1925, that Rupp died on August 22 at Beth-El Hospital after having lived in Monument for more than thirty years.

Figure 23: Gravestones of:

Mary K. Rupp,
Block 6 Section 9 N1

Dr. Rupp,
Block 6 Section 9 S2

## The Guires
### Pioneers Who Survived the Perils of Homesteading

The August 28, 1960, *Colorado Springs Gazette-Telegraph* states that Henry Guire, his wife, Mary Ann, and their children, along with his brothers David, Jake, and Josiah, headed for the Colorado Territory in 1864 by covered wagon. The article states that Mary Ann traveled with her "Democratic Rose and sunburst quilts and her Marriage Pledge of 1854, decorated by Henry's pen knife with hearts, flowers, birds and trees." The article also said they brought two milk cows, tied behind the wagon, and Mary Ann "would milk the cows and put some of the milk in containers at the rear of the wagon. The jolting of the wagon soon churned it into fine butter."

The article described the troubles they encountered during their long journey west:

**Figure 24: Henry and Mary Guire later in life**
*Courtesy of the Palmer Lake Historical Society*

> Henry drove on ahead so that he might find a location for his family, leaving them with the others to follow. On selling his flour [in Denver], he learned of the dreadful massacres in

Nebraska, and fearing for the safety of his wife and children, he hurried to join them. Fortunately they were safe. The wagon train they were with had remained in Fort Kearney, Neb., for a few days to make repairs and escaped the fate of the wagons which had been ahead and behind them. The people and stock had been killed and the wagons burned.

In the spring of 1865, Henry Guire and his family homesteaded near David and Catherine McShane. Between 1870 and 1890, brothers Henry, Jacob, Joseph, David, and Josiah Guire homesteaded in El Paso County, near Monument. As was the tradition of the time, Henry Guire's homestead papers were signed by President Ulysses S. Grant.

Henry and his family built an eight-room, two-level house with the help of neighbors. It was made of stone with two-foot-thick walls. The walls were plastered inside and outside with the dual purpose of insulation and protection from Native American attacks.

One day, Mary Guire saw Native Americans approaching her home. She hid her children and then, according to the *Gazette-Telegraph* article:

> One of the braves stalked into the kitchen and demanded that she give him matches. She told him she had none.
>
> "Heap big lie!" the Indian yelled, pointing at a box on the window sill. Immediately, he fitted an arrow to his bow. Mary Ann snatched up a flat iron from the stove and started to hurl it at him. The Indian ducked and backed out the door, crying "Heap brave squaw!" The next minute he joined his companion, and they rode away."

The Guires' wagon train included David McShane, and it

Figure 25: Grave markers of Mary (left) and Henry (right) Guire, Block 14 Section 1 N1 and N2

is believed that the Guire brothers helped him build his fort. The Guire name is on the fort's plaque.

Mary Guire died on January 22, 1894, and Henry followed her on February 23, 1899. The Guires have two of the more recognizable grave markers in the cemetery. They are shaped like tree trunks.

David Guire died on July 23, 1902. The July 24, 1902, *Colorado Springs Gazette-Telegraph* carried Guire's obituary, saying he was politically a Democrat and that he attended the Dunkard Church. It praised his business ethics and his important role in area agricultural development and said that he "contributed much to the advancement and improvement here and aided in laying broad and deep the foundation upon

**Figure 26:** Grave marker of David C. and Nancie Guire, Block 17 Section 12 S2 and S3

which has been built the present prosperity of the district."

Like other Monument pioneers, David Guire was present during the 1868 Indian uprising. His obituary stated that he was "active in fighting and subduing the red men, who went upon the warpath, murdering and pillaging and burning the homes of many of the settlers."

The death of David Guire, unfortunately, was gruesome. A July 24, 1902, *Rocky Mountain News* headline stated, "Body Mangled: Old Pioneer of Monument District Killed While Crossing a Railway Track." Guire was killed by a Denver & Rio Grande passenger train while crossing the tracks on July 23. Both his horses were also killed, and his wagon was smashed to pieces. Guire is buried with his wife, Nancie, who had died thirty years before him.

## John Olfs
### Atheist Turned Believer

John Olfs was born in Holstein, Germany, on December 26, 1841. Linda Case wrote in her June 18, 2020, *Tri-Lakes Tribune* column that Olfs immigrated to the United States in 1860 and homesteaded 160 acres outside Monument. He married his wife, Christine, in Denver on November 28, 1872. *The Castle Rock Journal* reports that nearly ten years later, on April 26, 1882, Olfs "purchased the farm of Mr. McShane which joined Mr. Olf's place."

Figure 27: The Olfs homestead. Pictured are Hannah Olfs Maulsby, her son Raymond, Christine Olfs, and her son Frank.
*Courtesy of the Palmer Lake Historical Society*

Figure 28: Gravestones of:
Baby Harry Hagedorn (left) with two of the four trees John Olfs planted, Block 7 Section 1 N1
John and Christine Olfs (right), Block 6 Section 12 N1

Olfs was Lucille Lavelett's grandfather. When his first grandchild, Harry Hagedorn, died in 1895 at the age of two and a half, Olfs dug up four pine trees from his homestead (now the site of the Woodmoor Barn) and planted them at the corners of the boy's grave. Lavelett wrote in her book that Olfs claimed to be an atheist. But, he said, "If these four trees grow, I'll know there is a God in Heaven, and little Harry is in Heaven." All four trees survived. Two of them are still standing behind Harry's grave.

John Olfs died on July 24, 1898. He is buried with his wife, Christine, who outlived her husband by sixteen years.

## Paton Wilson
## Civil War Vet Turned Potato Farmer

According to the September 23, 1889, *Rocky Mountain News*, the first "plowing for potatoes on the divide was done by the late John Russell, in the spring of 1862." Russell "sold the potatoes for $22 per 100 at the cellar, and $26 per hundred at Denver. He realized $11,000 for the fifteen acres of potatoes."

In 1877, Paton Wilson of Monument grew twenty-five thousand pounds of potatoes per acre, at a time when the average per-acre yield was four thousand to six thousand pounds. Some of the potatoes were huge, weighing more than three pounds and measuring up to twenty-seven inches.

Before potato farming, Wilson served from 1861 to 1865 as

Figure 29: Potatoes grown in Monument, Colorado, circa 1908
*Courtesy of the Palmer Lake Historical Society*

a private in the Eighth Regiment, Iowa Cavalry, Company E, as part of the Union Army. According to the website Roster and Records of Iowa Soldiers, Wilson of Mount Pleasant, Iowa enlisted on July 18, 1863, at the age of eighteen. His regiment took part in the successful Battle of Resaca, where the South yielded ground to Major General William Sherman. Wilson was taken prisoner on July 30, 1864, in Newnan, Georgia during the Battle of Brown's Mill when Union

Figure 30: Gravestone of Paton Wilson, Block 1 Section 1 N1

general Edward McCook made a daring raid to sever the South's communication and supply lines but was defeated by Confederate general Joseph Wheeler. Wilson mustered out on June 5, 1865, in Clinton, Iowa.

Paton Wilson married Margaret Alice Kendall in Colorado Springs on December 29, 1874. Wilson died in Monument on June 30, 1894. The July 3, 1894, *Rocky Mountain News* reported on his death, saying that he died of heart disease, "leaving a wife and six children."

There is some discrepancy on the spelling of his first name. It's spelled "Paton" on his gravestone and in the obituary in the *Rocky Mountain News*, but the cemetery ledgers list him as "Patton" and the Roster and Records of Iowa Soldiers website lists him as "Paten." The spelling on his gravestone is assumed to be correct.

## Mary E. Doyle
## The Ice King's Mother

Mary Short married William Doyle. Their son William E. Doyle was born in 1865. They moved to Pueblo and by 1884, the W. E. Doyle & Company, a butchery, was advertising beef, pork, mutton, poultry, and other meats. Eventually the family moved to the Monument area. On January 19, 1901, *The Rocky Mountain News* reported that "Messrs. Hanks and Doyle began to cut ice on the Monument reservoir today." Doyle and Thomas A. Hanks had leased the reservoir, and begun work on a new ice house, built of wood from the nearby Black Forest.

Figure 31: The Doyle Ice & Storage Company, circa 1930
*Courtesy of the Palmer Lake Historical Society*

**Figure 32: Ice blocks loaded into train cars, circa 1920**
*Courtesy of the Palmer Lake Historical Society*

The two men ran Monument's ice harvesting business, supplying blocks of ice to the local community. On February 7, 1902, *The Castle Rock Journal* reported that they had the contract to furnish the Denver and Rio Grande Railroad with five thousand tons of ice and were shipping six carloads daily.

According to Lavelett's book, "In ice harvest days, the winters were COLD! From the first of November, Monument could always plan on the weather to range from 10- to 20-below zero every night." *The Colorado Springs Gazette* describes ice harvesting in Colorado in a November 20, 2023, article:

> For several weeks in winter, upward of 50 men are hired and join horses to cut and pack ice on sawdust. They make 40 cents per hour, according to the historical society. Thousands of tons are stored and sold to homes and businesses.

> Ice from the Monument reservoir was cut into blocks by horse-pulled grooving knives. The horses then hauled the blocks into the icehouse, where it was packed in twelve inches of straw. The ice was eventually loaded onto railcars bound

Figure 33: Cutting ice blocks from the Monument reservoir
*Courtesy of the Palmer Lake Historical Society*

for Denver and Pueblo. Workers labored seven days a week. Monument stopped harvesting ice in 1943. Monument's

Figure 34: Mural celebrating Monument's ice harvesting history, located on the corner of Second Street and Beacon Lite Road

ice harvesting is memorialized in artwork designed by Tim Upham and Lisa Cameron in a collection of reverse-painted acrylic blocks. It's located on the water treatment building at the corner of Second Street and Beacon Lite Road.

Mary Doyle died on April 17, 1911.

Figure 35: Gravestone of Mary Doyle, Block 6 Section 4 N1

## Charles D. Ford
## Monument's Hotelier

On September 21, 1878, reporters wrote in *The Colorado Springs Gazette* about their visit to the Monument Hotel:

> At 11 o'clock a. m. we rode into the town of Monument. A description of this charming little village would be out of place with our pen, its beauties of location and scenery being too well known. With the true instinct of a newspaper man, we found ourself heading for the *Mentor* office, where we received a most cordial welcome from Mr. A. T. Blatchley, ye editor. We gladly accepted the invitation to make his sanctum our headquarters, and after a short visit we passed across the street to the Monument Hotel where we found dinner in readiness.

Figure 36: Advertisement from the August 16, 1882, *Castle Rock Journal* for the Monument Hotel, showing C. D. Ford as proprietor

We were really surprised to find a hotel of this kind in a town the size of Monument. It is both large and well built, the rooms large and well ventilated. There are nineteen sleeping rooms all furnished in a tasty manner, with the best furniture and carpets. Aside from these is an elegant parlor and office of no mean pretensions, and adjoining the latter a cosy and comfortable reading room. Here a person can enjoy all the hotel privileges, together with the comforts of home. The proprietor, Col. F. R. Ford, is from "way down in Maine," and as we heard a

Figure 37: Monument Hotel
*Courtesy of the Palmer Lake Historical Society*

Figure 38: Colonel Francis R. Ford and his wife, Henrietta
*Courtesy of the Palmer Lake Historical Society*

gentleman remark, "is a born landlord." . . . The dining room and culinary departments have the personal supervision of Mrs. Ford, whom we found to be a lady with rare qualities for the position she occupies. . . . The charges are extremely moderate, being only $2.00 per day with a generous reduction by the week.

Colonel Francis Ripley Ford, and his wife, Henrietta, were some of Colorado's earliest pioneers, with the colonel arriving in 1859. In 1860, Henrietta and her children, twelve-year-old Charles and his fourteen-year-old sister, traveling from Maine in a Concord coach, arrived in Colorado. The Fords homesteaded a claim west of Monument and in 1870 built the Monument Hotel.

The July 10, 1902, *Rocky Mountain News* reported that Henrietta Ford "built the Monument Hotel and managed it profitable while her husband F. R. Ford was engaged in mining." The newspaper went on to say that Mrs. Ford and her family "made four trips across the country to and from Maine, traveling part of the way by wagons, as the railroads had not [been] built west of the Missouri River."

Henrietta Ford lived in Monument for thirty years, until her death on July 10, 1902. She and her husband are both buried in Denver.

Charles eventually took over the running of the hotel from his parents. After him, the proprietors were Roy and Nellie Petrie.

A fire destroyed the hotel on March 24, 1922. The destruction of the hotel was reported in the March 25, 1922, *Colorado Springs Gazette*. The newspaper article stated that the fire "started in the east section of the building and rapidly enveloped the structure." Hotel guests were awakened by smoke and the sound of the fire roaring through the main hall. The guests watched the hotel, and their personal belongings, burn. The article reported that no effort was made to stop the blaze. Luckily, there was no wind that day, so the fire didn't spread to other buildings.

Charles Ford married Anna Bradford. He died in 1926, one year before his wife.

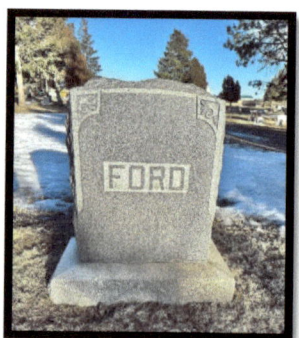

Figure 39: The Ford family headstone (center) with individual markers for Charles and his wife, Anna,
Block 1 Section 6 S2 and S3

## John W. and Emily Higby
## Monument Business Owners

John William Higby was born on February 17, 1854, to John William Higbee and Catherine Anstine. It is unknown why John changed the spelling of his name from "Higbee" to "Higby." On January 10, 1877, he married Emily Marie Briley, and in 1888 he moved his growing family to Eastonville, Colorado, where he worked as a clerk for the Russell-Gates Mercantile Company.

According to Higby's biography, published in Wilber Fisk Stone's *History of Colorado*, in 1888 Higby "homesteaded one hundred and sixty acres and also preempted a similar amount

Figure 40: Mr. and Mrs. J. W. Higby, from Stone's *History of Colorado*, 1919

**Figure 41: The Higby dry goods store in Monument**
*Courtesy of the Palmer Lake Historical Society*

of land and secured a timber claim of like size near Calhan, Colorado." To take ownership of the land, the homesteader had to "prove it up," meaning they had to make improvements and live on the property for five years. As John Higby was working in Eastonville at the time, it was left to Emily Higby to homestead the land alone.

In 1900, Higby moved to Monument and established the Higby Mercantile Company, located where the Chapala Building now stands at the corner of Second and Washington Streets. His biography states that he "held to the highest standards in the personnel of the house, in the line of goods carried, in the treatment of his customers, and his business showed a rapid and substantial growth."

The Higby Mercantile Company safe still sits in Covered Treasures, a bookstore located in the old building. Covered

# SHOOTOUTS, KILLINGS, AND WAR HEROES

Figure 42: The Chapala Building which currently houses the Covered Treasures bookstore

Figure 43: Safe that originally belonged to the Higby Mercantile Company

Treasures owner, Tommie Plank, says the safe has never been opened since she's been there and currently there are no plans to open it.

In 1902, the Higbys bought 1,640 acres of woodland near Monument, where John built several sawmills. He used this acreage to cut fifty-thousand ties for the Denver & Rio Grande Railroad. In 1910, he bought a 16,280-acre ranch in Greenland, where he lived until his death.

Higby's biography states

Figure 44: Historical plaque on the Chapala Building honoring the Higby family

that "on his deathbed [he] desired it to be known that to his wife he owed his success in life, saying that any man with a wife like his could not do otherwise than win success, for she at all times was the guiding spirit of his life, encouraging and assisting him when there were trials and difficulties to be met."

John Higby died on February 14, 1916. Emily outlived him by twenty-five years, dying on July 25, 1941.

Figure 45: Gravestones of John and Emily Higby, Block 4 Section 11 S1 and S2

## Fred Simpson
## The Lion Killer

Fred William Simpson was born in El Paso County on May 15, 1879, to pioneering parents Albert Balaam Simpson and Sarah M. Roberts. He was a farmer, carpenter, and superintendent of the Doyle Ice & Storage Company.

He is best remembered for his 1922 shooting of a huge mountain lion, nicknamed Old Disappearance, which had been killing livestock in El Paso County for years. The October 28, 1922, *Denver Post* reported that the lion was eight feet, two inches long and weighed 160 pounds. The article stated that

Figure 46: Fred Simpson with his dog Rover and the mountain lion Simpson killed
*Courtesy of the Palmer Lake Historical Society*

**Figure 47:** October 28, 1922, *Denver Post* reporting of Simpson's killing of Old Disappearance

the lion was estimated to be more than fifteen years old and that in the previous few months the "hungry lion has killed more than thirty calves."

Simpson spent more than three hours chasing the lion and killed it with a .22 caliber rifle after his dog forced the animal up a tree. He earned a bounty of $25 offered by *The Denver Post*. He had the lion stuffed and mounted, and it was later donated to the Palmer Lake Historical Society. It can be seen at the Lucretia Vaile Museum in Palmer Lake. Every time someone passes by the lion, a recorded roar goes off.

Simpson married three times. The first time was to Maudie Wilson on November 21, 1906. She died in 1917. Two years later, on New Year's Eve 1919, he married Ruby Blake Hunter in Denver. That marriage ended in divorce about eight years

Figure 48: Old Disappearance in the Lucretia Vaile Museum in Palmer Lake

later.

Simpson married his third wife, Golda Leona "Goldie" Flowers, in 1934. She was Monument's postmaster from May to September 1942. She was also among the inaugural members of the Monument Cemetery Association, serving as Treasurer.

Fred and Goldie were married for twenty-seven years until Fred's death on January 3, 1961. Goldie died thirty-two years later, on May 14, 1993.

Figure 49: Grave markers of Fred Simpson and his wives Maudie and Goldie Simpson, Block 5 Section 5 N1 and N2

## James Newbrough
## World War II Hero

James Walter Newbrough was a great-grandson of David McShane. He was born in Monument on February 15, 1921 and married LaJoye Marie Culver on October 25, 1948. Like many other men of his age, he fought in World War II, joining the army in September 1942. He became a hero during the July 31, 1943, Munda Air Strip Battle on the island of New Georgia in the South Pacific.

The October 17, 1943, British edition of *Yank* magazine highlighted Newbrough's bravery during the battle of New Georgia, where he was credited with saving his battalion.

On July 31, 1943, Private Newbrough's unit, the 1st

Figure 50: This picture of Private James Newbrough was featured in the October 17, 1943, British edition of *Yank*.

battalion, 161ˢᵗ infantry regiment, had been cut off on the island of New Georgia in the South Pacific. The article described the battle and Newbrough's bravery:

> On the right-flank center was a light machine gun with both gunners gone, one sick and the other momentarily absent at the start of the attack. Manning the gun was the ammunition carrier, a sandy-haired, drawling buck private named James Newbrough of Monument, Colo.
>
> When the attack started Newbrough was on the gun. A Jap in front of him yelled, "Americans cowards!"
>
> "The hell you say," Newbrough snorted.
>
> "Come on out and fight," yelled the Jap, tossing a rock.
>
> "Come on in and get me," said Newbrough. . . .
>
> As the fight progressed Newbrough, alone on the gun, kept it going constantly. Nobody, not even he, knows how many belts of ammunition he expended. As the gun continue to fire, it attracted more and more attention until it seemed that Newbrough was the only target. Bullets splattered into everything, cutting down the shelter half on top of him and clearing the underbrush from around him.
>
> Newbrough unfastened the traversing mechanism and, crouching low, sighted along the under side of the barrel so that no part of him was above the level of the gun itself. With his hand over his head he hung onto the trigger and raked the ground before him.

For his heroism during this battle, Newbrough was awarded the Silver Star with an oak leaf cluster. The Silver Star is the third-highest US Military award, given exclusively for combat valor. He was also awarded two Bronze Stars for action on Guadalcanal.

Figure 51: Headstone of James W. Newbrough, Block 3 Section 3 S2

Newbrough died on July 12, 1983.

## Moses F. Chandler
## Monument's First Blacksmith

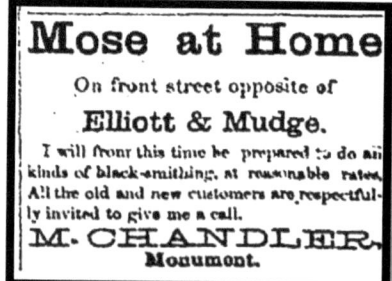

Figure 52: Chandler's advertisement of his blacksmith business in the October 12, 1881 *Castle Rock Journal*

Moses Chandler was an early Monument pioneer. He married Alice Costin on November 10, 1873, at Henry's Station. He bought town Lots 7 and 8 from Henry B. Walker in 1878. He was Monument's first blacksmith, doing work for the county in 1877 and advertising his business in the local newspaper.

Like many pioneers, he needed numerous occupations

to survive. On August 16, 1882, *The Castle Rock Journal* announced that "Mr. M. Chandler, the blacksmith of this place, has secured the services of two capable men to take care of his establishment. He has about 120 acres of grain to cut." Chandler was also an inventor who in 1887 was issued a Colorado patent for a seeding machine.

Although there is little information about Chandler, newspapers did carry interesting tidbits about his life. The April 5, 1893, *Castle Rock Journal* reported the following:

> The house of Moses Chandler near Monument was destroyed by fire last week. Mr. Chandler has been peculiarly unfortunate as this is the fourth time his house has been destroyed by fire since he has been on his present farm. Nothing was saved.

Moses's wife, Alice, died in 1915. After her death, Moses moved to Portland, Colorado and lived with his daughter, Mrs. Hugh Jones. He died a year later and was buried beside his wife in Monument Cemetery.

**Figure 53:** Gravestone of Moses and Alice Chandler, Block 8 Section 9 S2 and S3

## Alonzo Welty
## The Oldest Known Grave in the Cemetery

Almost nothing except his gravestone marker is known about Alonzo Welty. The headstone indicates that he died in 1860, twenty-six years before Charles Bissell donated the land for the cemetery. Lucille Lavelett wrote that the land Bissell donated had been used as an unofficial town burial site since 1871, but Welty died before any known homesteaders settled in the area.

Welty's gravestone is a curious mystery. It is believed to be constructed of fairly modern material, not of 1860 vintage. The oldest dated headstone in Monument Cemetery leaves more questions than answers, and a quest for another researcher.

Figure 54: Alonzo Welty's gravestone,
Block 1 Section 8 N1

## CHAPTER 4

# Memorial Day in Monument

Memorial Day in Monument was not the big event it is today. At the first Memorial Day ceremony author John Howe attended in 2011, he was joined in the cemetery by only about fifty people. Residents Kelly and Lucy McGuire stood by the flagpole and talked to the crowd about the veterans buried in the graveyard. There are

Figure 55: Gravestone of Civil War veteran A. B. Simpson of the Third Regiment, Colorado Cavalry, Company B, Block 19 Section 4 S2

Figure 56: Marker of World War I veteran Benjamin C. Marston, Block 15 Section 10 S2

more than 130 veterans from all branches of the military in Monument Cemetery, including those who served in the Civil War, World Wars I and II, Korea and Vietnam.

Howe and Sharon Williams, the town gardener, worked

Figure 57: Headstone of Glenn F. Melton, US Army, World War II, Block 11 Section 9 S2 1

Figure 58: Memorial Day, May 29, 2023. Members of St. Peter Church, Knights of Columbus Assembly #2594, Knights of Columbus Assembly #11514, American Legion Post 9-11, and VFW Post 7829 raised, then lowered, the American flag and the POW/MIA flag.

to make the ceremony bigger, better, and more inclusive. They enlisted Boys Scouts, Girls Scouts, veterans, and a diversity of religious representatives to participate. They also invited political leaders to speak and added an opening

Figure 59: Memorial Day, May 29, 2023, with Palmer Ridge High School graduate Michael Carlson playing taps

Figure 60: Gravestones of veterans
William Joseph Austin, Block 19 Section 2 S3, and
William Theodore Crenshaw, Block 16 Section 4 N1

prayer and a final blessing. Within a few years, crowds increased dramatically. In 2024, about four hundred people attended.

Some of the veterans' files included information about their service provided by Barbara Neilon, the librarian at Benet Hill Monastery in Black Forest.

**FRANCIS M AGNEW**

**Born:** about 1847, Georgia
**Died:** 9 Dec 1886
**Married:** Ella Walker
**Units:** Bugler, enlisted as private in Company M, Kansas 5th Cavalry Regiment, 5 Oct 1863
Transferred to Company B, Kansas 15th Cavalry Regiment. These units fought in skirmishes primarily in Arkansas, and to protect the Kansas border.

By 1880 Francis & Ella with 3 young children, Minnie, Earl and Maud were living in El Paso County, CO. Francis was a "sawmill man" possibly employed by William Bassett who operated a sawmill in the western part of the "Pineries," now known as Black Forest.

Figure 61: Grave of Francis M. Agnew, Block 19 Section 3 N1, and information gathered by Barbara Neilon, Benet Hill Monastery librarian

**CHAPTER 5**

# Large and Unusually Shaped Gravestones

Unlike some cemeteries, Monument Cemetery places no restrictions on the size or shape of a gravestones. The only regulation is that the monument or marker

Figure 62: Marker of slain siblings Ryan Charles Willhite and Scarlett Christine Gallagher who were laid to rest in the same casket.
Block 5 Section 2 N3

Figure 63: The Tucker family headstone, Block 15 Section 8 N1, N2, and N3

be placed six inches inside the burial plot, and that the head of the deceased is faced toward the west. As a result, there is a wide variety of shapes and sizes throughout the cemetery. This chapter shows some of the more unusual headstones in the cemetery.

Figure 64: Marker of Hiram Martin "Randy" Chamberlain, Block 12 Section 8 S1

# Shootouts, Killings, and War Heroes

Figure 65: Headstone of Carol M. and K. Charles H. Kleeberg, Block 5 Section 7 S1

Figure 66: Graves of Sylvia Gorball (left), Block 2A Section 8 N3, and Jennie G. Bishop (right), Block 19 Section 6 S1

Figure 67: Gravestones of Joshua Singh (above), Block 9 Section 5 N2, and Shirley and Paul Edward Ducommun (below), Block 2 Section 6 S1

**CHAPTER 6**

# Cemetery Visits

Over the years, we made several trips to Monument Cemetery to gather information or confirm material we had found in our research. We would also take photos of headstones for the cemetery files. These trips helped us become familiar with the names of the deceased, burial locations, and styles of tombstones.

Sometimes maps indicated the location of a flat gravestone, also called a grass marker, but we found nothing there. These types of stones tend to sink below the surface over time. We would dig around to see if we could uncover the marker. Sometimes we noticed an empty space between graves, which indicated that someone should be buried there, but no stone was visible.

We would have to start poking around, hoping we didn't poke into anything unpleasant. We would take a pointed probe and stick it in the ground in several locations until we heard a *thunk*. Then we would start digging.

Figure 68: Authors John Howe (left) and Michael Weinfeld (right) poking around Monument Cemetery
*Courtesy of the Tia M. Mayer Collection*

We got on hands and knees and carefully dug with trowels to discover what was there. Sometimes it was just a rock, but if it was a gravestone, we would unearth it and raise it to ground level. Passersby might well have thought we were grave robbers.

We didn't think there was any danger of accidentally discovering remains. As far as we knew, there were no natural burials in the cemetery, and remains were normally buried at least six feet deep.

There are several reasons for deep burials. Burying a body deep in the ground prevents odors that might attract animals or be unpleasant for nearby neighbors. Deep burials also make it harder for grave robbers, who might steal body parts or valuables. Finally, burying a body deep reduces the chance of spreading diseases.

```
STATE BOARD OF HEALTH OF COLORADO
          BUREAU OF VITAL STATISTICS
   Paso    BURIAL OR REMOVAL PERMIT           No..........
ity..................              Date of Death......7-21-27............., 19....
      Colorado Springs
Full Name...Hamilton W. Bennett............Age..72-11-13..Sex..male....Color..white
Disease Causing Death..........Carcinoma of Prostate...............................
Place of Burial...................................................................
  or
Removal to......Monument, Colo..................via...auto.........................
Undertaker......D. F. Law Co................Address....Colorado Springs, Colo......
   A certificate of death having been filed in my office in accordance with the laws of Colorado, I hereby
 uthorize the......removal.........of the body of said deceased person, as stated above
           (Burial or Removal)                                    [signature]
        7-21-27                                          (Registrar's Name)
..........................., 19....                      District No....6..
```

## CHAPTER 7

# Who Is Right?

Throughout our research, we discovered numerous contradictions between the gravestones and official documents. Whenever we ran into this problem, we had to scour historic records, search historic Colorado newspapers, find documents from the Colorado Board of Health, and visit with experts at the Palmer Lake Historical Society. Some of our hardest detective work involved the graves of Vilna Helton, Hamilton Bennet, the two John Munsons, Clarrisa Barry, and Vergal Charles Bishop. The results from our research are shown on the following pages.

# Shootouts, Killings, and War Heroes

## Vilna France Sly Helton
### Died: January 14, 1984
### Location: Block 16 Section 5 S1

Is her name spelled "Vilna" or "Vilma"?

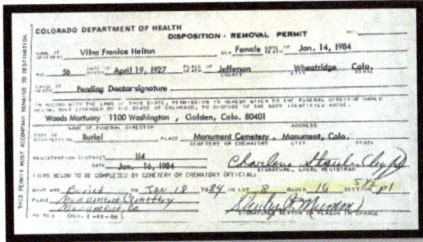

"Vilma" on her headstone    "Vilna" on her death certificate

**Obituary:** *Daily Freeman Journal*, Webster City, IA - Mar. 2, 2006

Lloyd C. Helton, 87, of Webster City, died Tuesday, Feb. 28, 2006 at the Southfield Wellness Community. A Gathering will be held at 10:30 a.m. at the Foster Chapel, with sharing of memories by family and friends. Burial will be at a later date at the Monument Cemetery at Monument, Colorado. Military rites will be conducted by American Legion Post # 191 of Webster City.

Lloyd Charles Helton, son of Ivan and Esther Graham Helton, was born March 20, 1918, the oldest of nine children, at Mercer, MO. He received his education at Mercer and Princeton, MO. He spent some of his younger years in the Davis City, area. In his youth, he was a Golden Gloves Champion Boxer. During W.W. II, he served with the Iowa National Guard-U.S. Army-Headquarters Company-3rd battalion-133rd Infantry (Red Bull) Division in the European, African and Middle Eastern Theatres of Action. He received 3 bronze stars and was honorably discharged in 1945. Following his discharge, he was married to Vilna France Sly on May 14, 1945 at Olathe, KS. The couple farmed near Leon for 10 years, then Hansel for 8 years. The family moved to Webster City in 1964 and he worked at Christeson Auto Sales and Service for 16 years. They retired in 1982 and moved to Colorado. He worked part-time at the Foreign Auto Body at Denver, Co. Mrs. Helton died January 14, 1984. He returned to Webster City in 1985. Since July of 2003, he had resided at Southfield.

**We believe Vilna is the correct spelling.**

## Were There Two John Munsons?

We found two different headstones with the name John Munson. In addition to the two headstones, there were two burial files, The burial location, birth date, and death date were the same in each file. One file contained a photo marked 1901, and we found records of a John Munson who died at birth in 1901. The other file contained a certificate that showed John Munson was crushed to death by a coal car in a mine, but we didn't know where his body was located.

## Were There Two John Munsons?

We searched through several old maps and finally found the location of the second John Munson.

Above: the baby John Munson who died at birth,
Block 5 Section 12 N3

Below: the adult John Munson who died in a mining accident,
Block 4 Section 11 N3

**Monument Cemetery has two different John Munsons.**

# Vergal Charles Bishop
## Died: October 25, 1933

Was his name spelled "Virgil" or "Vergal" Bishop?

His name is spelled "Virgil" on his death certificate.

His gravestone spells the name "Vergal" Bishop, Block 2 Section 12 N2

**A check of the 1930 US Census indicates that the headstone spelling is correct.**

# Shootouts, Killings, and War Heroes

## Clarrisa Barry
### Died: January 3, 1930
### Location: Block 6 Section 2 S3

Was her name Clarissa J. Berry or Clarrisa J. Barry?

**STATE BOARD OF HEALTH OF COLORADO**
BUREAU OF VITAL STATISTICS
BURIAL OR REMOVAL PERMIT

County: El Paso
Town/City: Colorado Springs
Date of Death: 1-3-30
Full Name: Clarissa Janet Berry
Age: 85 yrs  Sex: female  Color: white
Disease Causing Death: Lobar Pneumonia
Place of Burial or Removal to: Monument, Colo
via: auto
Undertaker: Decker & Son   Address: Colorado Springs

Dated: 1-3-30
District No. 69

Her name is spelled "Clarissa J. Berry" on her death certificate.

On her headstone and in our ledger, her name is spelled "Clarrisa Barry."

**Since our ledger matches her headstone, we believe her headstone reflects the true spelling of her name.**

# Hamilton W. Bennet
## Died: July 21, 1927
## Location: Block 5 Section 3 S1

Was his name spelled "Bennet" or "Bennett"?

It is spelled with two *t*'s on his death certificate and with one *t* on his headstone.

His brother was Hiram P. Bennet, Colorado's first delegate to Congress. We believe one *t* is correct.

# CHAPTER 8

# Iron Fences

Some family plots are surrounded by iron fences. According to cemetery committee minutes, the fences were installed to protect graves from wandering cattle.

There are two styles of fences in the cemetery. One style was made by the Hassell Iron Works Company of Colorado Springs and the second was made by Stewart Iron Works of Covington, Kentucky.

Figure 69: Emblems of the Hassell Iron Works (left) and the Stewart Iron Works (right) on the fences at Monument Cemetery

Figure 70: A Monument Cemetery fence built by the Hassell Iron Works Company

Hassell Iron Works Company was started by William Hassell, who like many early pioneers, came to Colorado seeking a cure for his tuberculosis. His oriental ironwork fence business dominated the fence industry in the Pikes Peak region. Stewart Iron Works, founded by Richard Clayborne Stewart Sr. in 1862, was by the turn of the twentieth century "the largest ornamental fence company in the world, employing more than seven hundred workers," according the company website.

Stewart Iron Works created all the benches in New York's Central Park and was also responsible for the light fixtures at the US Capitol in Washington, DC, and the gates at the Panama Canal. In 1902, the company spun off a new division, the Stewart Jail Works Company. This division provided cells for federal

Figure 71: The prison cells at Alcatraz Federal Penitentiary
*Image courtesy of the Stewart Iron Works Company*

penitentiaries in Leavenworth, Kansas; Sing Sing Correctional Facility in New York; and Alcatraz in California.

Figure 72: A Monument Cemetery fence built by the Stewart Iron Works Company

Figure 73: Stewart Iron Works Company bench in New York's Central Park (left) and Stewart Iron Works Jail Division plaque (right)
*Images courtesy of the Stewart Iron Works Company*

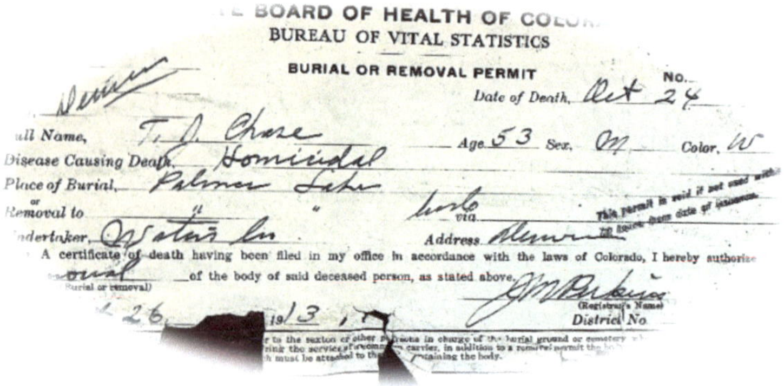

BOARD OF HEALTH OF COLO...
BUREAU OF VITAL STATISTICS
BURIAL OR REMOVAL PERMIT
No.
Denver
Date of Death, Oct 24
...ull Name, T. J. Chase Age 53 Sex, M Color, W
Disease Causing Death, Homicidal
Place of Burial, Palmer Lake
or Removal to " " auto via
Undertaker, Waters Co. Address Denver
This permit is void if not used within ... from date of issuance.
A certificate of death having been filed in my office in accordance with the laws of Colorado, I hereby authorize burial of the body of said deceased person, as stated above.
(Burial or removal)
...26 1913
(Registrar's Name)
District No.

# CHAPTER 9

## Unusual Causes of Death

While researching the cemetery files, we found several unusual causes of death. One certificate listed "imbecile" as a cause of death.

Psychiatrists once used the term *imbecile* to describe people with moderate to severe intellectual disability. How the condition could contribute to someone's death was not explained in the certificate. Along with *imbecile,* the death

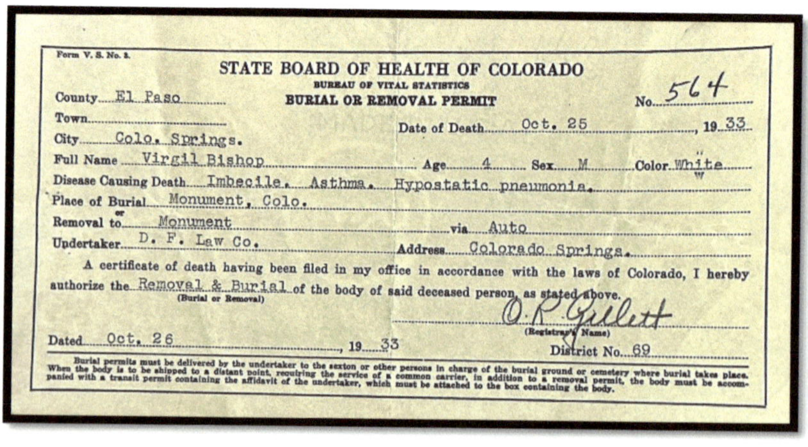

Form V. S. No. 5.
STATE BOARD OF HEALTH OF COLORADO
BUREAU OF VITAL STATISTICS
BURIAL OR REMOVAL PERMIT
County El Paso No. 564
Town
City Colo. Springs. Date of Death Oct. 25, 1933
Full Name Virgil Bishop Age 4 Sex M Color White
Disease Causing Death Imbecile. Asthma. Hypostatic pneumonia.
Place of Burial Monument, Colo.
or Removal to Monument via Auto
Undertaker D. F. Law Co. Address Colorado Springs.
A certificate of death having been filed in my office in accordance with the laws of Colorado, I hereby authorize the Removal & Burial (Burial or Removal) of the body of said deceased person, as stated above.
O. R. Gillett (Registrar's Name)
Dated Oct. 26, 1933 District No. 69
Burial permits must be delivered by the undertaker to the sexton or other persons in charge of the burial ground or cemetery where burial takes place. When the body is to be shipped to a distant point, requiring the service of a common carrier, in addition to a removal permit, the body must be accompanied with a transit permit containing the affidavit of the undertaker, which must be attached to the box containing the body.

**Figure 74: Death certificate of Vergal (name misspelled on certificate) Bishop listing "imbecile" as cause of death**

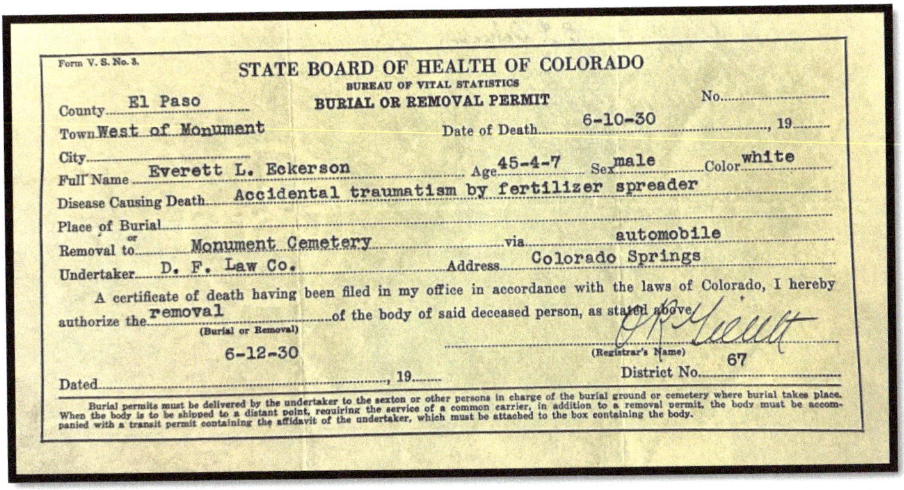

Form V. S. No. 3.

STATE BOARD OF HEALTH OF COLORADO
BUREAU OF VITAL STATISTICS
BURIAL OR REMOVAL PERMIT

No.

County El Paso

Town West of Monument

Date of Death 6-10-30, 19

City

Full Name Everett L. Eckerson Age 45-4-7 Sex male Color white

Disease Causing Death Accidental traumatism by fertilizer spreader

Place of Burial or Removal to Monument Cemetery via automobile

Undertaker D. F. Law Co. Address Colorado Springs

A certificate of death having been filed in my office in accordance with the laws of Colorado, I hereby authorize the removal (Burial or Removal) of the body of said deceased person, as stated above.

(Registrar's Name) O R Gillett

Dated 6-12-30, 19

District No. 67

Burial permits must be delivered by the undertaker to the sexton or other persons in charge of the burial ground or cemetery where burial takes place. When the body is to be shipped to a distant point, requiring the service of a common carrier, in addition to a removal permit, the body must be accompanied with a transit permit containing the affidavit of the undertaker, which must be attached to the box containing the body.

**Figure 75: Death certificate of Everett Eckerson listing cause of death as "accidental traumatism by fertilizer spreader"**

certificate listed asthma and hypostatic pneumonia as cause of death.

The cause of death on another certificate was listed as "accidental traumatism by fertilizer spreader." According to the June 13, 1930, *Record-Journal* of Douglas County, Everett Eckerson died after being "run over by a manure spreader." The article states:

> There were no eye witnesses of the accident, but it is believed that Eckerson, who had just hitched a team of horses to the spreader, attempted to adjust something on the harness and in some manner frightened the teams, which started up, throwing him to the ground. Two wheels of the spreader passed over him, one across his chest and the other passing slightly lower, across the abdomen.

Eckerson is buried beside his children: Clarence Willard, who died in childbirth on January 18, 1918; Flora, who died four months before her third birthday; and Everett Lawrence

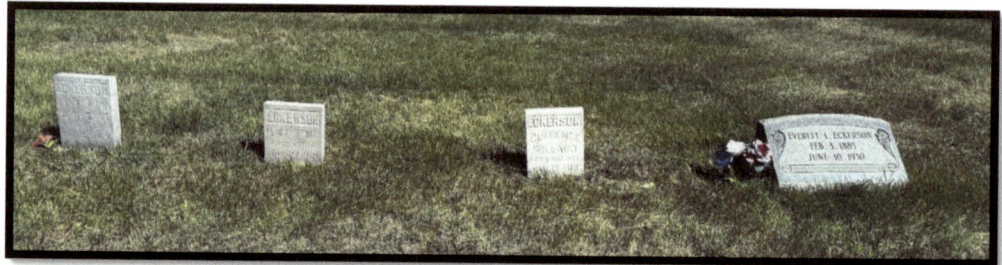

**Figure 76: Gravestones of Everett Eckerson and his three children, Block 5 Section 6 N1-4**

who died in childbirth on August 15, 1919.

On October 24, 1913, T. J. Chase was listed with a cause of death as "homicidal." It is assumed this is a mistyping of "homicide" since Chase's obituary, published on October 31, 1913, states that he was "shot, Friday morning, in Denver." The article lists him as a "kind and loving husband and father," giving no indication that he was homicidal.

A man named Harry Hillen, whom the media dubbed "the boy bandit," was convicted of murdering Chase in the first degree by a jury in district court in Denver on December 17,

Form V. S. No. 3.

STATE BOARD OF HEALTH OF COLORA[illegible]

BUREAU OF VITAL STATISTICS

BURIAL OR REMOVAL PERMIT

County, Town, City, Denver

No.

Date of Death, Oct 24 1913

Full Name, T. J. Chase Age 53 Sex, M Color, W

Disease Causing Death, Homicidal

Place of Burial, Palmer Lake

or Removal to " " via

This permit is void if not used within ... hours from date of issuance.

Undertaker, Waters Co Address Denver

A certificate of death having been filed in my office in accordance with the laws of Colorado, I hereby authorize the Removal (Burial or removal) of the body of said deceased person, as stated above.

(Registrar's Name)

Dated Oct 26 1913 District No.

[illegible] must be deliv[illegible] to the sexton or other persons in charge of the burial ground or cemetery where burial takes place. When [illegible] carrier, in addition to a removal permit the body must be accompanied with a transit [illegible] must be attached to the [illegible] containing the body.

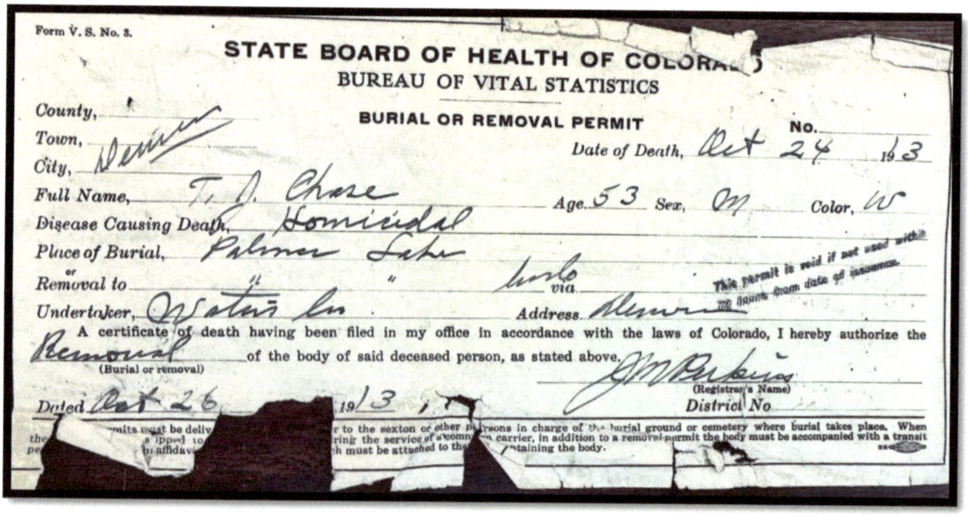

**Figure 77: Death certificate of T. J. Chase with "homicidal" given as cause of death**

**Figure 78:** Gravestone of Thomas J. Chase, Block 13 Section 7 S2

1913. Hillen was sentenced to hang.

*The Weekly Courier* reported on October 31, 1913, that Hillen was a twenty-two-year-old waiter in downtown Denver. He was accused of some fifty robberies, including at stores and homes and stickups. *The Longmont Ledger* reported on July 2, 1915, that Hillen, "with a mysterious friend known as 'Curley,' planned crimes and procured revolvers." During the week of October 20, 1913, the two held up scores of men. *The Ledger* reported that Hillen "murdered Thomas Chase, a Denver real estate man, in cold blood because Chase 'smiled at him' and 'didn't move fast enough to suit him.'"

The *Rocky Mountain News* of October 28, 1913, quoted Hillen as saying:

> A bandit is born and not made. The kind that learn to be crooks, real crooks, are found only in moving pictures. I have committed over fifty crimes, but never yet have harmed a woman. I don't like them but I respect them. I killed Thomas J. Chase because he snarled at me. I can't stand snarls. It was the snarl of a bartender that caused me

to make the gun-play that put me in the hands of the cops.

According to the December 12, 1913, *Herald Democrat*, Hillen testified at his trial that the confession was coerced by police using "threats and abuse." But the district attorney testified that Hillen willingly signed the confession, admitting "here goes my death warrant."

Hillen was hanged at the state penitentiary in Cañon City, Colorado on June 24, 1915. He reportedly maintained his innocence to the end.

Other causes of death found on death certificates include:

- Accidental automobile traumatism
- World War II
- Enlarged tonsils
- Syphilis of the brain
- Burned in a house fire
- Accidental overdose of aspirin
- Cerebral hemorrhage from falling out of a streetcar
- Skull and jaw fracture from a car crash
- Fractured skull from a car-truck collision
- Fatal skull fracture from a train crash
- Removal of gall bladder
- Asphyxia from inhalation of helium gas
- Gunshot wound to the head
- Extensive burns (accidental)
- Freezing

**CHAPTER 10**

# Other Interesting Discoveries and Information

Several death certificates list causes of death that only a doctor would understand. We looked them up trying to understand what they would mean today. Some of the more interesting include:

- Facial erysipelas, an infection of the skin
- Cancer of the cecum, a cancer at the very beginning of the colon
- Total atelectasis, or deflation of the alveoli, causing a collapsed lung
- Phthisis, an old term for tuberculosis.
- Bright's disease, a kidney disease that today is called acute or chronic nephritis
- Cholelithiasis, or gallstones in the gallbladder.
- Inanition, which is defined as "exhaustion caused by lack of nourishment." In other words, the victim starved to death.

Many of the deceased had first names that are no longer popular. These include:

| | |
|---|---|
| Oskaloosa | Okalona |
| Melvina | Orpha |
| McPoumroy | Savery Livery |
| Elva | Elvera |
| Elvessa | Oria |
| Vida May | Vella |
| Vilna | Standley |
| Geneva | Merlin |
| Maudie | Zelpha |
| Benony | Arthelia |
| Charity | Hopwood |
| Phineas | Gertha |
| Wilmot | Zenophen |
| Nelda | Manna |
| Josiah | Otha |

There are no real celebrities in Monument Cemetery, just some well-known locals. However, some of the deceased share names with celebrities. We have a Jack Kennedy, two Judds (Anna and Frank), a Howard Johnson, an Anna (not Anne) Frank, a Paul Peterson (not the one from *The Donna Reed Show*), a Justin Hayward (not the singer with the Moody Blues), a John Walsh (not the host of *America's Most Wanted*), and a Fred Krueger (not the character from *Nightmare on Elm Street*).

# Shootouts, Killings, and War Heroes

Figure 79: The gravestone of "celebrity" Fred Krueger, Block 11 Section 2 N1 1

We call this a "loose history" of the cemetery because there remain many gaps in meeting minutes as well as unexplained inconsistencies in the ledgers and maps. This is the most complete history we could write at the present time.

One thing we noticed when poring through the records is that many people, including coroners, employees of the state health department, and officials who signed death certificates, often misspelled "interred" as "interned."

Monument Cemetery was designed so that all the graves would be in a row and the headstones would face west. Unfortunately, this isn't the case for many of the graves.

We thought it humorous that the cemetery did business with an excavating contractor named "Ray's Diggin's."

One death certificate said, "Always write in black ink." It was written in aqua ink. One man's records of relatives were lost in the Chicago fire of 1871.

In 2005, a woman contacted the town to see if her great-grandparents were buried here. Our ground-penetrating radar indicated that there are two unmarked graves next to her grandparents, so those might be her great-grandparents.

While writing this book, we met once a week in the town

hall office of Tina Erickson. (She was deputy town clerk when we started and has since been promoted to town clerk.) That is where the nearly two thousand cemetery files are kept, as well as the ledgers, maps, and other information we needed to complete our project.

We hope you enjoy reading our book as much as we enjoyed researching and writing it.

Figure 80: John Howe at our worktable. Notice the bag of chocolate in the middle of the table. That is what kept us going!

CHAPTER 11

# Cemetery Timeline with Significant Dates

The following timeline has been constructed from various sources including the cemetery committee and association minutes, town of Monument cemetery reports, correspondence from *Our Community News* (Monument's monthly all-volunteer newspaper; John Howe is on the newspaper board, and Michael Weinfeld is an editor there), and Lucille Lavelett's *Through the Years at Monument, Colorado*. There are gaps where no minutes or information were recorded (and some information was omitted for space.)

### May 28, 1886

Charles R. Bissell, originally from New York, sold five acres of land to the Town of Monument for $1 to be used as a cemetery. As with other documents from this time, Bissell's name is spelled two different ways on the deed (sometimes with a single *l* and sometimes with a double *l*.)

Charles Bissell began advertising as a physician and

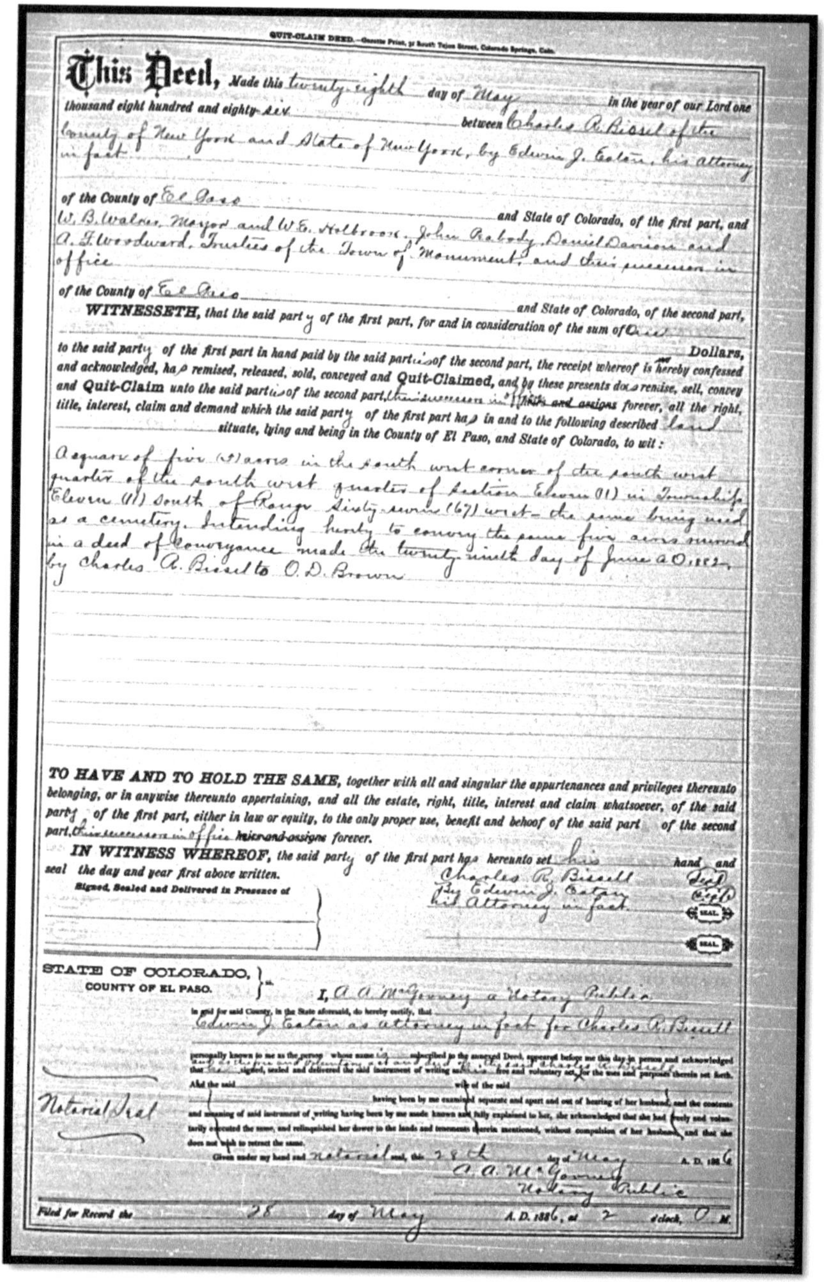
QUIT-CLAIM DEED.—Gazette Print, 31 South Tejon Street, Colorado Springs, Colo.

This Deed, Made this twenty-eighth day of May in the year of our Lord one thousand eight hundred and eighty-six between Charles R. Bissell of the County of New York and State of New York, by Edwin J. Eaton, his attorney in fact,

of the County of El Paso and State of Colorado, of the first part, and W. B. Walker, Mayor and W. E. Holbrook, John Peabody, Daniel Davison and A. T. Woodward, Trustees of the Town of Monument, and their successors in office

of the County of El Paso and State of Colorado, of the second part,

WITNESSETH, that the said party of the first part, for and in consideration of the sum of One

to the said party of the first part in hand paid by the said parties of the second part, the receipt whereof is hereby confessed and acknowledged, has remised, released, sold, conveyed and Quit-Claimed, and by these presents does remise, release, sell, convey and Quit-Claim unto the said parties of the second part, their successors in office forever, all the right, title, interest, claim and demand which the said party of the first part has in and to the following described land situate, lying and being in the County of El Paso, and State of Colorado, to wit:

A square of five (5) acres in the south west corner of the south west quarter of the south west quarter of Section Eleven (11) in Township Eleven (11) South of Range Sixty-seven (67) west - the same being used as a cemetery. Intending hereby to convey the same five acres named in a deed of Conveyance made the twenty ninth day of June A.D. 1882, by Charles R. Bissell to O. D. Brown

TO HAVE AND TO HOLD THE SAME, together with all and singular the appurtenances and privileges thereunto belonging, or in anywise thereunto appertaining, and all the estate, right, title, interest and claim whatsoever, of the said party of the first part, either in law or equity, to the only proper use, benefit and behoof of the said part of the second part, their successors in office forever.

IN WITNESS WHEREOF, the said party of the first part has hereunto set his hand and seal the day and year first above written.

Signed, Sealed and Delivered in Presence of

Charles R. Bissell [Seal]
By Edwin J. Eaton
his attorney in fact.

STATE OF COLORADO, COUNTY OF EL PASO.

I, A. A. McGovney a Notary Public in and for said County, in the State aforesaid, do hereby certify, that Edwin J. Eaton as attorney in fact for Charles R. Bissell personally known to me as the person whose name is subscribed to the annexed Deed, appeared before me this day in person and acknowledged that he signed, sealed and delivered the said instrument of writing as his free and voluntary act, for the uses and purposes therein set forth.

Notarial Seal

Given under my hand and notarial seal, this 28th day of May A.D. 1886
A. A. McGovney
Notary Public

Filed for Record the 28 day of May A.D. 1886, at 2 o'clock, P. M.

Figure 81: Quit claim deed showing Charles R. Bissell sold the land that would become Monument Cemetery to the town of Monument on May 28, 1886

*Courtesy of the El Paso County Clerk and Recorder Steve Schleiker*

surgeon in *The Colorado Springs Gazette* as early as January 2, 1875. Unfortunately, our research found no information about why Bissell sold the land to the town. Local historian Lucille Lavelett wrote that the land had already been used unofficially for burials since 1871, although Alonzo Welty's 1860 headstone indicates that burials may have occurred earlier. Lavelett quotes a newspaper correspondent as writing, "Hither-to the dead were buried indiscriminately, no one having a lot and families have consequently become badly mixed."

### Summer of 1886

According to Lucille Lavelett, a well was dug at the cemetery. Water was obtained by a rope pulley and buckets and was used to water the grass and the flowers. Today, the cemetery uses town water.

### March 8, 1896

R. H. Ashworth surveyed and platted the cemetery. A sexton was hired at an annual salary of $5. A sexton is someone who looks after a graveyard, often acting as a gravedigger.

### 1898

According to Mayor Elizabeth Wiegers' Memorial Day speech of 1982, the cemetery was officially dedicated in 1898. Wiegers said, "We are fortunate indeed to have such a lovely setting. It is a sanctuary of peace and quiet with its full view of the Front Range, stately pines, and by one recent account, over 62 varieties of wildflowers." (A list of wildflowers was created in 1983 by Lela Hagedorn and is included later in this book.)

### October 1899

Deeds for cemetery lots cost $1. No deed was given for a

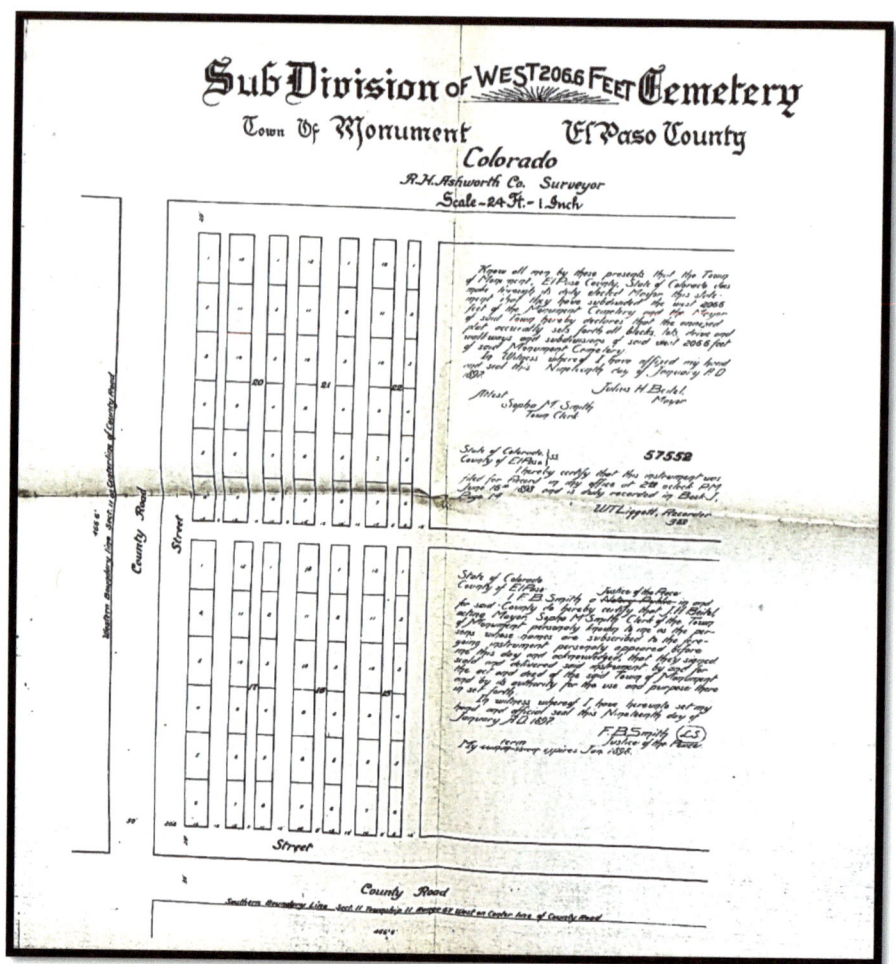

**Figure 82:** R. H. Ashworth's platting of Monument Cemetery

fraction of a lot.

### May 4, 1903

Jacob Geiger was named sexton to be paid $15 a year.

### April 11, 1904

Jacob Geiger donated his $15 sexton's salary for a new iron

## Shootouts, Killings, and War Heroes

gate that was bought on August 8. That gate was later stolen and had to be replaced.

A Mr. Curry was appointed cemetery caretaker, a job he held until 1929.

### August 14, 1909

A northbound Denver & Rio Grande train, operated by engineer O. H. Lessig, crashed head-on with a southbound passenger train, controlled by engineer W. H. Hollingsworth. This happened in what was then the town of Husted, around where the north entrance to the US Air Force Academy is today.

The January 25, 2022, *Tri-Lakes Tribune* reported, "The two

Figure 83: 1909 train wreck near the town of Husted
*Courtesy of the Palmer Lake Historical Society*

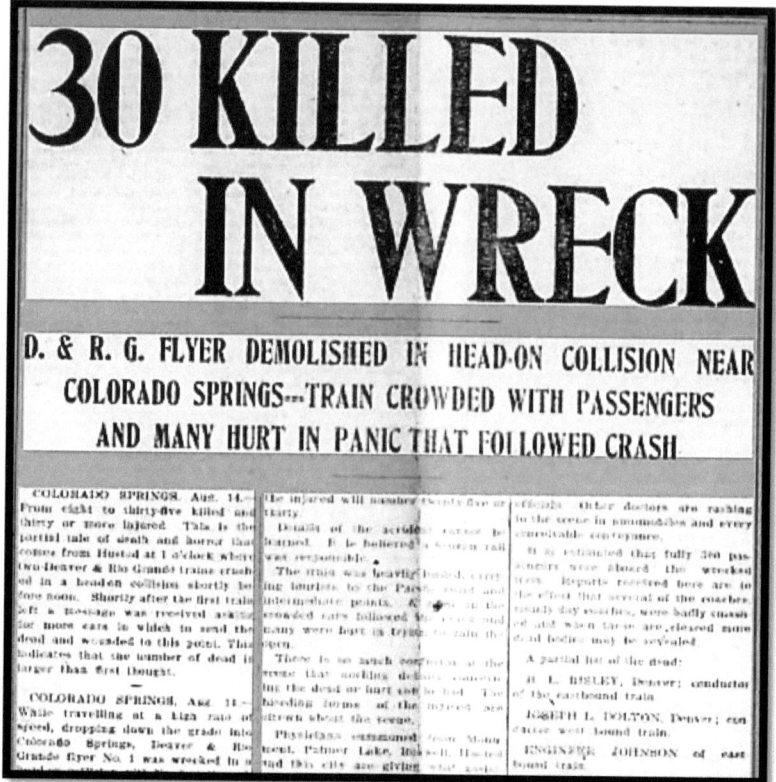

Figure 84: Headline and story on the front page of the August 16, 1909, *Durango Semi-Weekly Herald*

engines turned into a classic 'nose up' wreck and toppled over toward Monument Creek. The first car in each train was crushed behind their engines." Of the four hundred people on board the two trains, between twelve and thirty people died and more than sixty were injured.

Some of the dead were buried in Monument Cemetery as unknowns because in those days, people didn't carry the sort of identification we have today; some of the bodies were never identified.

The August 15, 1909, *Rocky Mountain Daily News* reported that Lessig "became frantic with grief as he gazed upon the dead and dying." The article stated that spectators saw Lessig try to kill himself by "leaping in front of an approaching train," but he was saved by four men.

Lessig was blamed for the accident. The October 29, 1909, *Delta Independent* covered his trial for manslaughter, which lasted only two days. The October 29, 1909, *Rocky Mountain News* reported that the jury deliberated for four hours before Lessig was acquitted. Some of the survivors of the wreck were in court to hear the verdict.

### Around 1916

According to Lucille Lavelett, Mrs. Bertha Curry was Monument Cemetery's last undertaker. Lavelett wrote in her book that Mrs. Curry would keep the body in the deceased's bedroom until burial. In the summer, the body would be surrounded by tubs filled with ice until the funeral.

Other Monument Cemetery undertakers included Will Lierd, John E. Smith, and J. F. Roth. All three men owned general stores that sold coffins.

Figure 85: Gravestone of Bertha Curry, Block 4 Section 8 N3

Figure 86: The store of J. M. Brown, formerly owned by Will Lierd
*Courtesy of the Palmer Lake Historical Society*

**A Bold Robbery at Monument**

MONUMENT, Colo., October 16.—A bold robbery was perpetrated here last night. The hardware store of J. F. Roth was broken into and a large amount of cutlery and other goods were stolen. The full moon was shining brightly and it seems almost incredible that some one did not either hear or see the robbers. An entrance was effected through a back window, the back door having been tried but could not be opened.

Figure 87: A robbery at the store of J. F. Roth as reported in the October 18, 1894, *Colorado Weekly Chieftain*

## 1918—1919

It is estimated that the 1918 Spanish influenza, which began near the end of World War I, claimed the lives of more than one hundred thousand soldiers. The pandemic also affected Colorado, with an estimated seventy-five hundred "excess

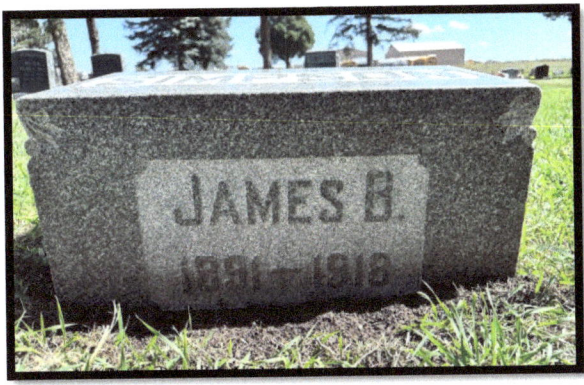

**Figure 88: Headstone of James Simpson, who died of influenza in 1918, Block 4 Section 8 N2**

deaths," according to the March 5, 2020, *Colorado Sun*. Monument Cemetery contains several individuals whose death certificate gives the cause of death as the "Spanish influenza."

Form V. S. No. 12.

STATE OF COLORADO
BUREAU OF VITAL STATISTICS
CERTIFICATE OF DEATH

PLACE OF DEATH
County of El Paso
Town of Monument Registration District No. 73
or
City of (No. St.; Ward)

File No. 1
Registered No. 17
[If death occurred in a Hospital or Institution, give its NAME instead of street and number.]

[If death occurs away from USUAL RESIDENCE give facts called for under "Special Information."]

FULL NAME James Blaine Simpson

PERSONAL AND STATISTICAL PARTICULARS

SEX Male COLOR White
DATE OF BIRTH Oct (Month) 10 (Day) 1892 (Year)
AGE 26 years, 14 months, days.
SINGLE, MARRIED, WIDOWED, OR DIVORCED Married
BIRTHPLACE (State or Country) Monument Colo
OCCUPATION Farmer
NAME OF FATHER A. B. Simpson
BIRTHPLACE OF FATHER (State or Country) Kentucky
MAIDEN NAME OF MOTHER Sarah Roberts
BIRTHPLACE OF MOTHER (State or Country) Mo
THE ABOVE STATED PERSONAL PARTICULARS ARE TRUE TO THE BEST OF MY KNOWLEDGE AND BELIEF
(Informant) A B Simpson
(Address) Monument Colo
Filed Oct 26 1919 W H Rupp Registrar

MEDICAL CERTIFICATE OF DEATH

DATE OF DEATH Oct (Month) 24 (Day) 1918 (Year)
I HEREBY CERTIFY, That I attended deceased from Oct 21 1918 to Oct 24 1918
that I last saw him alive on Oct 24 1918
and that death occurred, on the date stated above, at 8:30 AM
The CAUSE OF DEATH was as follows:
Spanish Influnza
Where contracted? (Duration) 3 Days
Contributory Pnemonia
Where contracted? (Duration) Days
(Signed) W H Rupp M. D.
Oct [illegible] 1918 (Address) Monument Colo

SPECIAL INFORMATION only for Hospitals, Institutions, Transients, or Recent Residents.
Former or Usual Residence How long at Place of Death ? Days

PLACE OF BURIAL OR REMOVAL DATE OF BURIAL
Oct 26 1918
UNDERTAKER ADDRESS
Andrew Curry Monument Colo

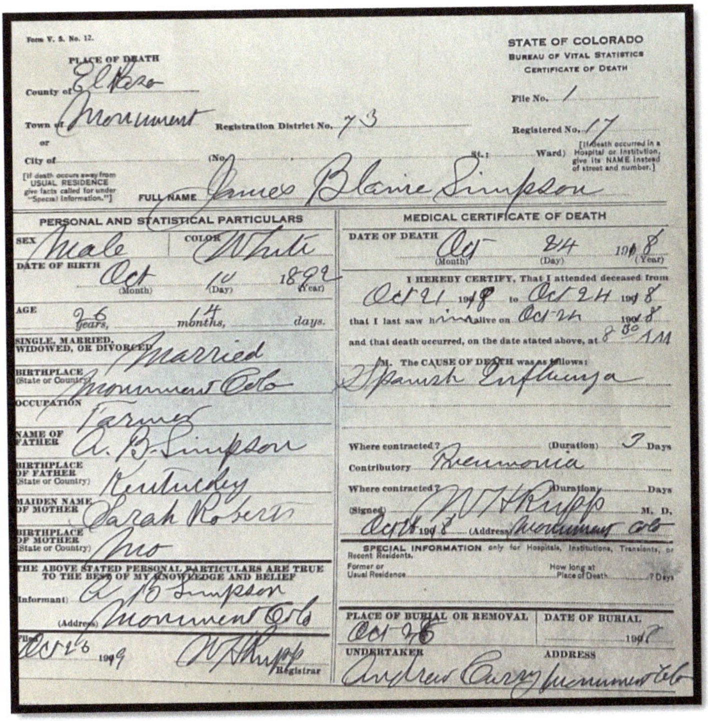

**Figure 89: Certificate of death for James Blaine Simpson, showing Spanish Influenza as cause of death**

### 1920 and After

Lucille Lavelett wrote that in 1920, Mrs. Ballou called a meeting to establish a committee to improve the cemetery. The committee included Ballou as president, J.A. Bougher as secretary, and William E. Higby as treasurer.

The committee sponsored High Five card parties, dances, and box suppers, raising money to install a woven vine fence. Climbing vines were attached to the metal fence on the east side of the cemetery. Before that, there was just a three-strand barbed wire gate. The fence's purpose was to hide the view of the adjacent vacant lot. Neither the vines nor the fence remain.

The committee was also responsible for buying a windmill, water tank, and platform for the southeast corner of the cemetery and water pipes and hydrants in the late 1920s and early 1930s. Also, the committee installed a double restroom in the cemetery. The work was done by ranchers and other community individuals who donated their time.

The Monument Homemakers Club served the volunteers lunches of hot dogs, potato salad, homemade pie, and coffee in the cemetery. Vandals later shot holes in the water tank and the windmill was torn down. Lavelett believed the vandalizing took place in the late 1940s or early 1950s.

The committee wrote to people who had moved away from the area, asking them for donations. Donations were also accepted at Memorial Day ceremonies. Lavelett wrote that the committee collected $200 one Memorial Day.

The committee also held chili-supper fundraisers.

### Late 1920s and Early 1930s

A group of evergreen trees was planted on the left side of the cemetery entrance as a memorial for Homemakers Club members. Five pine trees were planted east of the old well platform as memorials for five local men who died in World War I.

### November 14, 1922
The size of the cemetery increased when John A. Bougher sold forty-two feet of land on the east side from north to south for $1. Bougher is buried in the cemetery.

Figure 90: The gravestone of John Bougher, Block 1 Section 2 N1

### April 8, 1929
Phillip Hagedorn (Lucille Lavelett's father) was appointed cemetery caretaker.

**The authors were unable to find additional information about the cemetery from 1930—1939**

### 1940s
The town of Monument promised to take care of the cemetery, so the committee turned its funds over to the town. The town reportedly didn't keep its promise. Locust trees and lilac bushes took over the grounds which were never mowed.

### 1955
The cemetery was taken over by the town again.

**The authors were unable to find additional information about the cemetery from 1956—1967**

### Spring 1968
The Monument Cemetery Association was formed. The first members were President Margaret Plowman, Vice President Ethel Wissler, Secretary Dorothy Johnson, and Treasurer Goldie Simpson.

### 1968
Lucille Lavelett joined Margaret Plowman to clean up the

Figure 91: Left to right: Lucille Lavelett, Cemetery Association members Goldie Simpson, and Margaret Plowman, 1990.
*Courtesy of the Toni Martin Collection*

Figure 92: Historian Lucille Lavelett
*Courtesy of the Palmer Lake Historical Society*

cemetery. Lavelett wrote that the Monument Cemetery Association spent every Wednesday removing brush and digging out locust tree roots. The association persuaded the town to help with a backhoe to dig out the bigger roots and help with other heavy work. She said the association "caught plenty of hell," but it was worth it because the cemetery looked "so much nicer." This so-called beautification of the cemetery would eventually become a point of contention (see the entry for September 4, 1975).

Also in 1968, some graves were surrounded by iron fences to deter free-range cattle.

### 1972

The Monument Cemetery Association released a cookbook, which sold for $1, to raise money for the cemetery fund. It also thanked the Monument Hill Kiwanis Club for cleaning up the cemetery.

## 1975

A letter from Jerry McPhail, published on September 4, 1975, in *The Colorado Sun*, asked people to donate to the cemetery trust fund. Donations along with sales from cookbooks, provided for perpetual care at the cemetery. McPhail wrote "If every family would give $1.00 it would soon snowball into a fund that will really care for the Cemetery and for future generations to come."

## March 20, 1975

In a letter published in *The Colorado Springs Sun*, Mrs. Margaret Plowman stated that Mrs. Hattie Siehl had found children using the cemetery as a playground. She said they were climbing trees and setting fire to Mrs. Siehl's family gravesites. Mrs. Plowman said the fine for vandalism was $1,500. If the violators were children under seventeen, the parents would be held liable. Mrs. Plowman said the fence on the north side of the cemetery was down, but that wasn't how the kids got in there. (The fence had to be taken down while they got rid of the locust trees). Plowman wrote that children should not touch the flags on veterans' graves.

## May 26, 1975

Lunch was served before the meeting, and it earned $89.50, from which Margaret Plowman was reimbursed $11.01. Mildred Anderson made a motion that attorney James Weir be paid $90, the balance of his fee for establishing the trust fund. Goldie Simpson seconded the motion.

Mrs. Plowman said that many people had remarked about how much better the cemetery looked after she, Lucille Lavelett, Jerry McPhail, and the Monument Hill Kiwanis Club cleaned it up. (For a different perspective on their work, see the entry for September 4, 1975.) Lights were installed in the cemetery, but water for perpetual care was not yet available.

### July 9, 1975

The July 9, 1975, *Colorado Springs Sun* published a photo with the headline "Vandalism at town cemetery." The image showed the two stone markers of Henry and Mary Guire tipped over. Cemetery caretaker Ron Hilleman told police that an urn was also broken, and fresh flowers were removed from the grave. Police said it appeared there was more than one perpetrator because the stones and markers were so heavy.

Figure 93: Article about the July 9 vandalism, accompanied by a photo, published in *The Colorado Springs Sun*

### July 13, 1975

Monument Cemetery trustees met with members of the Monument Board of Trustees to discuss improving the cemetery.

The board said it wanted the trustees to coordinate with the newly formed Parks and Recreation Commission on future planning and solutions.

Mayor pro tem, Dr. Richard Beck, agreed that the cemetery had been in "direful neglect" (Mildred Anderson's words) and said he appreciated the renovation work done by President Plowman and Lucille Lavelett. Dr. Beck mapped out short- and long-range plans for the future of the cemetery. A list of priorities was drafted by the trust association.

### September 4, 1975

*The Colorado Sun* published an article with the headline "Cemetery facelift edged with brambles." It described the cemetery beautification project undertaken by a "self-appointed beautification committee."

The article, which went on to be titled "Cemetery facelift stirs controversy," stated that the beautification project was

Figure 94: Article published in the September 4, 1975, *Colorado Springs Sun* describes the controversy of the cemetery beautification project

so divisive that the two Lavelett sisters were no longer speaking to each other. The article stated:

> The commotion centers on a question concerning the dead: Should the Monument Cemetery remain a dilapidated but "charming" country graveyard, or should it be renovated into a "modern-style" cemetery with an irrigated, manicured lawn?

The article complained that "the town's maintenance crew began removing wrought-iron fences and concrete rims surrounding gravesites and yanked out some lilac shrubs and locust trees." The idea was to remove what some would call obstructions and others would call ornamentations to make mowing the lawn easier.

Opponents of the clean-up said they wanted the cemetery to look the way "their ancestors intended it." They claimed that no one consulted them before the clean-up started and that the "renovation has been sloppy, with breakage of concrete bases of tombstones, toppling of at least one gravemarker and damage to artificial flowers."

The head of the beautification committee, Margaret Plowman, told the paper, "Some people have the idea that just because they buy a (burial) plot it's theirs and they can leave it in bad condition." She said the cemetery needed to be leveled off so the lawn could be mowed. She said she couldn't imagine people wanting their loved ones "buried in a bunch of weeds."

One woman quoted in the story complained that a "willow tree was removed with no concern for the fact that her great-grandparents, buried near the tree, had transported it across the plains from Iowa in 1864." Another woman accused the committee of acting like "the Gestapo." A town trustee said descendants were given two weeks' notice of the planned alterations.

## September 11, 1975

Cemetery Association Trustee Mildred Anderson wrote to *The Colorado Sun* to express her "disgust" at the article from September 4, 1975. She said, "I deeply appreciate the efforts of restoring that historic old cemetery to its original beauty." She said no one had ever "destructively removed wrought-iron fences." In fact, she said, in one instance they had paid for rewelding a fence already destroyed.

She blamed "night marauders" for having "maliciously driven cars or motor bikes into iron posts, bent iron fences," and knocked down and broken old markers. She said the cemetery had become a "den of iniquity" with liquor bottles, remains of bonfires, and "filth," not to mention "orgies." Anderson said the paper should write about the people who have cared enough to restore the cemetery.

## October 5, 1975

An article in *The Colorado Springs Sun* said the Monument Board of Trustees would consider an ordinance that would give the town the authority to take charge of cemetery renovations. The proposal was a result of complaints about the "beautification" project that had angered some pioneer families. Some families wanted their ancestors' gravesites to be exempt from the proposed ordinance, which would prohibit railings, hedges, fences, and other "obstructions" that some families were trying to preserve. They said the style of their family gravesites dated back to 1874 and that's what their ancestors had wanted. Cemetery Association President Margaret Plowman said she thought the ordinance was a "splendid idea" that would result in a "permanently beautiful cemetery, with not everybody doing as they please."

### November 10, 1975

Mayor Luther Slabaugh said that upkeep of old-timers' graves would eventually fall back on taxpayers. A Mrs. Daniels said she wanted their graves left as is, saying that sixty people from her family were buried in the cemetery. Mrs. Carl Campbell suggested that each one be assessed for cleanup.

### June 18, 1976

Minutes from the Monument Cemetery Trust meeting showed a balance in the treasury of $1,038.80, after adding $136.80 in dues and gifts and $11.16 interest.

A Mrs. Larson, the caretaker, was complimented on the condition of the cemetery. It was suggested that a sign be erected showing the following list of rules to be observed:

- Plants only six inches around the stone
- No shrubs or trees on graves
- No plants on the graves
- Cars must stay on the established roadways

Lucille Lavelett made a motion that Margaret Plowman meet with the cemetery trust lawyer to determine how to incorporate the trust with the town's cemetery department. It was determined that the town needed to create a legal permanent fund so that perpetual care could be assured when a plot was purchased. It was suggested that an additional $60 be charged for perpetual care on top of the $65 cost of a plot. If the money was added to the trust fund, adequate principal would ensure sufficient interest to pay for a caretaker and other things needed to maintain the cemetery. (Note: There were many similar proposals for a perpetual care fund over the years. Each time it was thought that accumulating interest would pay for upkeep of the cemetery. The fund never came to fruition.)

### October 20, 1977

Sales of cookbooks netted $6.00. The treasurer reported an additional profit of $16.19, with $1 applied to the cemetery fund. The following rules and regulations for the cemetery were discussed:

- Gates should be open from 8:00 a.m. to 8:00 p.m. from summer to fall.
- The cemetery would be closed in the winter except for funerals or other services.
- Animals are not allowed in the cemetery.
- Cars are only allowed on designated roads.
- No firearms or fireworks except for military funerals.
- No defacing or destroying property.
- No fences or curbing.
- No flowers except in designated areas and by markers only.

The Board of Trustees requested that a contract between the Town of Monument and the Cemetery Trust be drawn up to protect the perpetual care funds of both parties. A fee of $40 per grave was proposed for residents, and $50 per grave for non-residents, for perpetual care to go into the trust fund.

### March 22, 1978

A Carol Owens investigated the possibility of renovating the old well in the cemetery. It was the consensus that a pipe should be added to the water line on the west side of the cemetery. The pipe would cost $62 per hundred feet, to be paid by the town cemetery budget.

There was a continuation of the discussion on the tentative agreement between the Cemetery Trust and the town of Monument. This was concerning the turning over of the trust's funds to the town for the establishment of a common perpetual care fund. In reviewing the agreement written by trust lawyer, James Weir, and approved by the town's lawyer, Thomas Cross, the board found several faulty clauses, and after lengthy discussions decided to present a new tentative agreement to the new Board of Trustees and presiding mayor after the election. Mrs. Plowman assigned the secretary to rewrite the agreement for the purposes of revision at a later meeting.

### September 29, 1982

What was known as Potters Field would now be the Crematory Garden. (It is not known what happened to those buried in Potters Field.)

### October 6, 1982

A design of the Crematory Garden was proposed, with a suggestion that all the markers there be flat. The burial of cremated remains on lots with an existing vault would be thirty inches deep. Two burials of cremated remains would be permitted, but only one stone or marker would be allowed. The committee discussed getting people who are fined by the town to work off their fines at the cemetery instead of paying the money in cash.

Figure 95: The Crematory Garden, 2024

## 1983 Cemetery Wildflowers
### (according to Lela Hagedorn)

- Lily of the Valley
- Harebell (spelled as Hair Bell)
- Larkspur
- Oxalis
- Spring Beauty
- Blue Daisy (on stem)
- Red and White Sweet Pea
- Canterbury Bells
- Fire Ball or Indian Pinks
- Red or White Honeysuckle
- Buttercups
- Soap weed
- Wild Rose (Pink or Red)
- Yellow Sweet Pea
- Bluebell
- Tiger Lily
- Flax (blue)
- Sand Spring Daisy
- Frost Daisy (purple)
- Buffalo Bean
- White Star Flower
- Yellow Daisy
- Sunflower
- Cactus (pink or red)
- Loco weed
- Tulip

# Shootouts, Killings, and War Heroes

| | |
|---|---|
| Sage (white bloom) | Live Forever |
| Sweet William | Anemone |
| Clover (red or white) | Sand Cherries |
| Lambs Quarter | Wild Currant |
| Lilacs | Catnip |
| Sweet Mary | Tansy |
| Bouncing Betty | Iris |
| Sedum | Hops |
| Woodbine | Willow |
| Spring Beauty | Columbine |
| Horse Mint | Sheep Sorrel |
| Wild Iris | Snap Dragon |
| Mullen | |

### June 1, 1983

The town of Monument honored Margaret Plowman with the Community Service Award for her efforts to make the cemetery "a truly beautiful place for our loved ones."

### March 22, 1989

The cemetery committee would like to find a way of keeping track of veterans for the cemetery log. One idea was to do so through a questionnaire when plots were purchased. Veterans flag holders are too expensive, so Caretaker Ron Hilleman would make flag holders and submit a bill for the cost to the committee.

Police will start locking gates at the cemetery with a combination lock and chain effective immediately.

Margaret Plowman made a motion to sell unidentified cemetery plots with no record of transactions in the cemetery log. The motion passed unanimously. Toni Martin made a motion to buy two new wooden trash containers and two whiskey barrels to be used as planters at the front gate for a price not to exceed $300. That motion passed unanimously.

## 1990
A *Tri-Lakes Tribune* article stated that Lucille Lavelett, Goldie Simpson, and Margaret Plowman were honored by the town for their efforts to clean up the cemetery. Plowman said that before their efforts the cemetery was "a joke and a disgrace." She said the lilac and locust bushes were "a great place for dope peddlers to hide their product."

## March 20, 1991
The possibility of forming a cemetery district was discussed. The group planned meeting where they would invite representatives from Palmer Lake, Woodmoor, and El Paso County. (Note: This was the first of many attempts to form a district that would help pay for cemetery upkeep. No district was ever formed.)

## June 1, 1992
According to the cemetery committee minutes, Chairman John Bailey said flowers had been planted, a broken headstone had been repaired, and the shed has been painted. Bailey said small granite headstones would replace tins on about eighty-five gravesites and would be acquired for under $1 apiece. He had spoken with someone who could sandblast the names and dates on them. Bailey felt he could keep the total cost under five dollars per headstone. He planned to get a sample to bring to the town hall for the committee to approve. He volunteered to install the headstones himself. The plaques on the benches would have additional engravings stating that they were donated by the cemetery trust.

Town Clerk Susie Haight said a cemetery district could be formed only by presenting a petition with signatures of fifty-one percent of the registered electors in the proposed district. This petition would have to be presented to the El Paso County Board of Commissioners. State statutes didn't provide for the formation of a cemetery district by an election. The committee would ask Brad Cowger to present the proposal for a cemetery district to the Tri-Lakes Ministers at their September meeting.

### November 8, 1993

According to Cemetery Committee minutes, Town Clerk Susie Haight reported on fees charged by other cemeteries. She said the town's fees were similar to, or higher than, others she had checked. The committee asked Haight to contact Lewis-Palmer High School to find a student willing to rake pine cones and pine needles at the cemetery.

Ron Hilleman had not noticed any vandalism in the cemetery. There was one headstone in need of repair. Hilleman would raise the flag on Veterans Day. John Bailey would try to obtain the stone for the small grave markers and give it to Toni Martin for cutting during January.

### March 14, 1994

Granite headstones for unmarked graves were a priority for the year, according to the cemetery committee. John Bailey would make sure the granite was still available. He volunteered to store it at his place of business. Toni Martin said her husband would help cut the stone. Town Clerk Susie Haight offered to contact local Boy Scout leaders to see if placing the stones on the graves would be a project they would be interested in as a troop, or if an individual working toward Eagle Scout would take on the project.

The committee would like help over the summer with watering flowers. Ron Hilleman offered to buy the flowers and Brad Cowger and his family offered to plant them.

Toni Martin expressed concern that the fence between the mobile home park and the cemetery was damaged again. Ron Hilleman said he would check on it. Toni Martin asked that the town call the owner of the mobile home park to ask him to repair the fence. Town Clerk Susie Haight offered to ask Dwight Whitney if the fence was a requirement of the approved plan, and whether she could contact them.

Margaret Plowman said she will start working on the arrangements for the Memorial Day service.

## April 18, 1995

Cemetery committee minutes reported that the Memorial Day service would be held May 29 at 10:00 a.m. Ron Hilleman would deliver flowers to Brad Cowger by May 22, and Cowger offered to plant them. Margaret Plowman has offered to get the information for the program to Town Clerk Susie Haight by May 8. Haight was responsible for getting the information printed and the programs back to Margaret. Haight also notified the *Tribune*. Ron Hilleman promised to install flags by the morning of the service.

There are about twenty-five headstones left for replacement of the metal markers. John Bailey has investigated getting the stone and having it pre-cut by the first week in May. Ron Hilleman planed to supply Toni Martin with a list of the names for the remaining stones.

The committee wanted the summer help to water flowers planted in the cemetery and to raise the granite markers that are below ground level. They also offered to repair the fence.

## September 12, 1995

The Cemetery Committee minutes contained the following

information. John Bailey, who was also on the Board of Trustees, announced he was resigning from the committee. Kristi Schutz, who was also on the Board of Trustees, offered to become the new chairperson of the committee.

The committee approved finishing and replacing the remaining granite grave markers (about 20). John Bailey planned to check the price of the stone and how much it would cost to cut it. Town Clerk Susie Haight plans to check into Boy Scouts wanting an Eagle Scout project. She also searched for someone to raise the stones installed last summer. They were set too low. The committee reviewed and approved the 1996 budget as presented.

## April 16, 1996

Cemetery committee members discussed finishing the replacement of the remaining granite grave markers (about twenty). Town Clerk Susie Haight was asked to check the price of the stone and how much it would cost to cut it and to have it engraved. The sign outlining the Cemetery rules needed to be replaced. Haight offered to get two bids and make sure it was done.

Ron Hilleman and Pat Patton planned to buy a new flagpole rope. The committee would like to have the front gate locked during evening hours. They would like the police department to make locking the gate part of their duties.

Margaret Plowman made arrangements for the Memorial Day service to be held May 27. Brad Cowger offered to make sure the flowers are planted.

## May 14, 1996

The Cemetery Committee unanimously approved Brad Cowger's motion to print Memorial Day programs. The wording World War I would be replaced with Veterans of

War to acknowledge the contributions of both World Wars.

Police Chief Al Karn told the committee he opposed locking the gate at night because it would make it more difficult for patrol officers to catch vandals. Instead, he assured the committee that he would have a patrol officer go through the cemetery twice a night.

Toni Martin expressed concern over headstones disappearing. Chairperson and Board of Trustee member Kristi Schutz read the report concerning the cost of cutting and engraving the headstones.

The committee also discussed having Mr. Spence raise the sunken headstones for up to $300. Brad Cowger submitted a motion to spend $1,375 to cut and engrave the headstones and added up to $300 for raising the stones. His motion was approved unanimously.

## April 14, 1997

The committee reported that staff worked on data entry of all cemetery records. They hoped to complete all data entry by the end of the year. The committee reviewed the Memorial Day programs and Brad Cowger volunteered to get the local ministers and the Boy Scouts to help with the service.

Trustee and committee chairperson Kristi Schutz suggested that the trees and bushes be trimmed before Memorial Day. Ron Hilleman offered to plant flowers at the cemetery before Memorial Day. Toni Martin said her daughter Amy would help plant flowers. Dale Hill was directed to get the time of the event published in *The Colorado Springs Gazette Telegraph*.

## December 9, 1999

The cemetery committee considered land for a new cemetery. Brad Cowger distributed a listing of properties for sale in the

Tri-Lakes area, including prices. Cowger said he would ask a real estate agent to help search for five-to ten-acre properties. In addition, he would contact another cemetery to find out how many graves could reasonably be dug per acre.

Town attorney Jim Folkestad said he would compile all the costs, submit them to the Town Manager, and ask him to decide whether it should be brought to the Board of Trustees for approval.

### December 20, 1999

Cemetery committee minutes reported that money for land for a new cemetery would come from the general fund, one mil for the land and one mil for the caretaker. Town attorney Jim Folkestad mentioned that we may be receiving some land for a cemetery from Forest Lakes as part of the annexation agreement.

### March 16, 2000

Town Manager Rick Sonnenburg said he spoke with Town Planner Patrick Mulready yesterday and the request for additional cemetery ground had already been presented to the Forest Lakes developer. The committee must wait to hear from them.

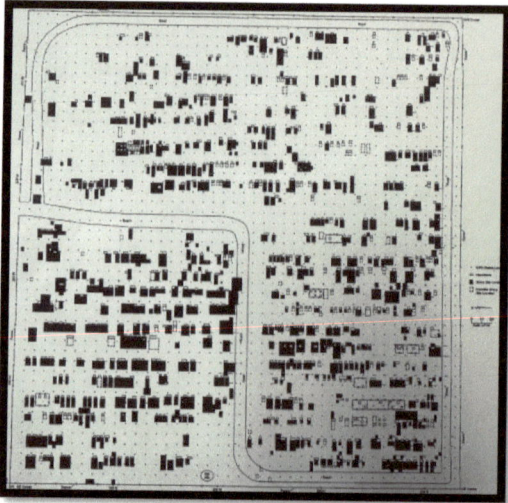

Figure 96: A worker using the ground-penetrating radar (left) and a resulting scan (right). The white squares on the scan indicate headstones. The black squares are gravesite locations, and the dotted lines indicate possible grave locations.
*Images courtesy of the GeoModel, Inc.*

## September 2001

The town hired GeoModel, Inc. of Leesburg, Virginia to use ground-penetrating radar at the cemetery. The company used a device that looked like a lawnmower to find unmarked graves. When the radar indicated something beneath the surface, the operator tried to determine if the object was a rock, a casket, shrouded remains, or something else. All remains were given plaster markers that said "unknown."

Figure 97: A plaster marker used to mark the remains found with the ground penetrating radar

The markers were made by Bob Schubert and Ray Fisk of the cemetery maintenance department.

### December 21, 2011

John Howe and Laura Nolt photographed all headstones and vacant areas and transferred the photos to a thumb drive which is now in a file marked "Photos" in the Town Clerk's office in the Town Hall.

### July 7, 2012

A cemetery report was published in *Our Community News*. Former Trustee Gail Drumm (who worked for a funeral home and cemetery in the past) was to present a committee report on the status of the finances and policies for the town's cemetery. The report included proposals on how to make the cemetery profitable in an era of increasing percentages of cremations by making a substantial investment in the purchase and installation of a columbarium. However, Drumm was not present as scheduled. Town Manager Cathy Green, Finance Assistant Sherry Jurekovic, and Trustee John Howe presented the report in Drumm's absence. Howe had been researching cemetery information for the committee for two years.

Town Clerk Cynthia Sirochman and former Deputy Town Clerk Claudia Whitney have assisted residents inquiring about the cemetery and reviewing and organizing about 100 years of cemetery records. Facts presented in the report included:

- There were typically ten to twelve burials per year.
- The cost of a plot was $800.
- The fee for opening and closing a grave site was $350.
- The average annual cemetery revenue for the previous

five years was $11,870.
- Estimated annual average direct costs for the previous five years of cemetery operation are $14,090 ($8,366 for labor and $5,724 for equipment).
- The average annual net loss over the previous five years is about $2,220, for a total of $11,102.
- Columbarium installations from Premier Columbaria ranged in price from $20,000 (240 niches) to $28,000 (312 niches.)
- Expanding the cemetery would cost about $80,000 per acre, with up to twenty vacant acres available on the opposite side of Beacon Lite Road.
- The current average cost for a funeral is about $10,000.

## April 2016

The Board of Trustees approved a project to replace 190 old plaster headstones marked "Unknown" with markers made of granite. Police detective Joe Lundy put John Howe in touch with Kent Griffith, who needed a project to earn his Eagle Scout badge.

Griffith met several times with his scout adviser who determined replacing the headstones would qualify as an Eagle Scout service project. Howe acted as the boy's project beneficiary representative for the town of Monument. Griffith told *The Tribune Extra* "This was a project that was really interesting to me with some history behind it and a high moral value." He coordinated with about thirty-five other volunteers, including other scouts, family members, and friends, to complete the work. He was required to replace fifty plaster markers with granite ones to earn his badge, but he and the other volunteers replaced 125 stones over two weekends in August.

Figure 98: One of the new granite headstones (left). Kent Griffith in front of a new granite headstone (right).
*Image of Kent Griffith courtesy of the Karen Griffith collection*

### October 2017

John Howe was presented with a white marble bench at the cemetery for the many hours he has spent updating and correcting the cemetery records and helping to organize the annual Memorial Day ceremonies. Howe joked, "as you can see, I am not beneath this bench." He added, "May this bench be a place for comfort and peace to those who come to Monument Cemetery." The bench is located east of Block 14.

### April 16, 2021

The last of the 1,692 plots was sold.

### April 25, 2024

John Howe and Michael Weinfeld were named Volunteers of of the Year by the Tri-Lakes Chamber of Commerce.

Figure 99: John Howe's marble bench (above). The presentation of Howe's bench in October 2017 (below).
*Photos courtesy of the Jim Kendrick Collection*

# Bibliography

## Books and Articles

Associated Press. "Shooter Had Problems at Christian Facilities," December 12, 2007.

Boster, Seth. "Frozen in Time: A Brief History of Ice Harvesting in Colorado." *Colorado Springs Gazette*, October 23, 2022, updated November 20, 2023.

*Boulder Daily Camera*. "Hillen, Bad Man, Dies on the Gallows," June 25, 1915.

Carrigan, Rob. "Ice Harvest in Monument." Restless Native, November 28, 2008. https://coloradorestlessnative.blogspot.com/2008/11/ice-harvest-in-monument.html.

Case, Linda Saulnier. "Monumental Happenings and Histories: Heroes among Us." *Colorado Springs Gazette*, June 11, 2019.

*Castle Rock Journal*. "Divide," April 26, 1882.

———. "Monument," February 7, 1902.

*Colorado Mountaineer* (Colorado Springs). "Murder at Monument," October 25, 1876.

———. "Real Estate Transfers," October 21, 1875.

*Colorado Springs Gazette*. "County Commissioners," November 10, 1877.

———. "District Court," March 3, 1877.

———. "Monument Hotel Burns in Early Morning Fire," March 25, 1922.

———. "Obituary: David Caylor Guire," July 24, 1902.

———. "On the Divide," September 21, 1878.

———. "Real Estate Transfers," August 31, 1878.

———. "Slain Siblings Mourned, Laid to Rest Together," February 22, 2013.

*Colorado Springs Sun.* "Cemetery Facelift Edged with Brambles," September 4, 1975.

———. "Vandalism at Town Cemetery," July 9, 1975.

*Daily Journal* (Telluride). "Mountain Lion Killed with .22 Rifle," November 4, 1922.

*Delta Independent.* "Husted Wreck Trial Begins," October 29, 1909.

*Denver Post.* "Guard's Hands "Didn't Even Shake" as She Shot Gunman," May 7, 2016.

———. "Monument Hunter Kills Lion, after Chase in Snowy Hills," October 28, 1922.

*Elbert Tribune,* "Foiled Savage Redskin: Death of Mrs. Isabella Trigg Recalls Thrilling Incident," November 3, 1904.

Emery, Erin. "Report Details New Life Church Shooting." *Denver Post,* May 21, 2016.

Feldman Memorial. "Why Are Graves Dug 6 Feet Deep?" Feldman Mortuary, September 6, 2022. https://feldmanmortuary.com/blogs/blog-entries/1/Blogs/25/Why-Are-Graves-Dug-6-Feet-Deep.html.

Freed, Elaine. "Colorado Springs' Historic Ironwork." *Americana Magazine,* May 1976. https://oldnorthend.org/wp-content/uploads/2012/02/Hassell_Iron-Works_Tour_FrontPage1.pdf

*Herald Democrat* (Leadville). "Hillen Says His Confession Result of Third Degree," December 12, 1913.

Lavelett, Lucille. *Through the Years at Monument, Colorado.* Palmer Lake, CO: Palmer Lake Historical Society, 2004.

*Longmont Ledger.* "Harry Hillen Dies on Gallows," July 2, 1915.

McGhee, Tom. "Church Shooter Wanted to Be Missionary." *Denver Post,* May 7, 2016.

———. "Father Remembers Two Daughters Killed at New Life Church," *Denver Post,* May 6, 2016.

McGrath, Maria Davies. *The Real Pioneers of Colorado,* vol. 1.

Denver: Denver Museum, 1934. https://history.denverlibrary.org/sites/history/files/RealPioneersColorado.pdf.

Morriss, Mack. "Infantry Battle in New Georgia." *Yank: The Army Weekly* 2, no. 18 (October 17, 1943). https://306bg.us/yank/yank17oct43.pdf.

*Out West* (Colorado Springs). "Notice: The Stock Owners of El Paso County," March 23, 1872.

*Palmer Lake-Monument News.* "Pioneers' Courage Eulogized as Fort Marker Is Dedicated," February 25, 1971.

Pikes Peak Genealogical Society. *Tombstone Inscriptions of the Monument, Colorado Cemetery.* Colorado Springs: Pikes Peak Genealogical Society, 2001.

*Record-Journal* (Douglas County). "Dr. E. L. Eckerson Killed near Monument," June 13, 1930.

———. "Monument and Divide," October 31, 1913.

*Rocky Mountain News* (Denver). "Across the Divide," February 25, 1874.

———."Another Foreign Fraud," December 31, 1879.

———. "Body Mangled: Old Pioneer of Monument District Killed while Crossing a Railway Track," July 24, 1902.

———. "Crops on the Divide," September 23, 1889.

———. "Death of Paton Wilson," July 3, 1894.

———. "Engineer Frantic at Sight Tries to Commit Suicide," August 15, 1909.

———. "Finished by November. The State Reservoir Near Monument Almost Completed," August 29, 1892.

———. "A Forger Brought Back from Kansas," January 30, 1878.

———. "In the District Court," February 13, 1880.

———. "Indians on Monument Creek," September 22, 1868.

———. "It Was a Success." September 23, 1891.

———. "Judge Elliott's Court," January 11, 1880.

———. "Late Colorado Patents," March 27, 1887.

———. "Lessig Acquitted of Blame for Wreck," October 29, 1909.

———. "Letter List," May 15, 1865.

———. "Mrs. Ford, Pioneer, Comes to Join Her Son," January 17, 1901.

———. "Pioneer of Monument Called to Last Rest," July 10, 1902.

———. "Potato Is King," September 18, 1891.

———. "Ruins Restored," September 7, 1902.

———. "To Utilize Ice of the Monument Reservoir," January 19, 1901.

Sabin, Marion Savage. *Palmer Lake: A Historical Narrative* Denver: Sage Books, 1957.

*Semi-Weekly Herald* (Durango). "30 Killed in Wreck," August 16, 1909.

Simpson, Kevin. "Aside from Some Quick Action in Gunnison, Cities and Towns across the State Struggled as the Flu Pandemic of 1918 Ran Its Deadly Course." *Colorado Sun*, March 5, 2020.

Stone, Wilber Fiske. *History of Colorado, Illustrated*, vol. 4. Chicago: S. J. Clarke, 1919.

*Tri-Lakes Tribune* (Monument). "An Awful 1909 Train Wreck in Colorado Springs," January 25, 2022.

*Weekly Courier* (Fort Collins). "Terror of Denver Confesses Guilt," October 31, 1913.

Wever, Peter C., and Leo van Bergen. "Death from 1918 Pandemic Influenza during the First World War. *Influenza and Other Respiratory Viruses* 8, no. 5 (June 27, 2014).

## Interviews and Archival and Web Materials

"About Stewart Iron Works." Stewart Iron Works, 2024. https://stewartironworks.com/about-stewart-iron-works.

Bureau of Land Management, https://glorecords.blm.gov. Federal land records for David, Henry, Jacob, and Joseph Guire and for Isabella Trigg.

"Butterfield Overland Dispatch Stage Stations." Legends of America, 2024. https://www.legendsofamerica.com/butterfield-overland-despatch-stage-stations/.

Case, Linda. Interviews with authors, 2024.

Curry, Andrew. Handwritten ledger entries, 1898–1925.

Family Search, family search.org. Material on Fred William Simpson (record LKVW-MY3), Moses Chandler (record G182-RLR), John William Higby (record LH1F-FJP), and Paton Wilson (record L693-72B).

"Forty-First Infantry." New York State Military Museum and Veterans Research Center. https://museum.dmna.ny.gov/application/files/7515/5060/0290/41st_Infantry_CW_Roster.pdf.

"Historical Sketch: Eighth Regiment Iowa Volunteer Cavalry." Iowa in the Civil War, 2024. https://iagenweb.org/civilwar/books/logan/mil608.htm.

Monument Cemetery. Handwritten records of lots sold, 1926–1953; handwritten record of burials, 1955–1989.

Monument Cemetery Association. Handwritten minutes.

Monument Cemetery Committee. Handwritten minutes.

Rathburn, Ron. Interview with authors, November 6, 2024.

Town of Monument. Cemetery reports, correspondence, original cemetery maps, records of lots and burials, 1925–1954.

Town of Monument website. Townofmonument.org.

# Acknowledgements

We would like to thank former Town Clerk Laura Hogan and current Town Clerk Tina Erickson for their help with this project. Laura oversaw the cemetery before Tina. Both were a major source of information for us. The records are in Tina's office, so she graciously let us share her space while we worked. She had to put up with our dark humor and constant chatter, some of which was actually about the work we were supposed to be doing.

We would also like to thank Town Council member Laura Kronick for suggesting that we turn our initial report on the cemetery into this book, as well as the rest of the Town Council and former Town Manager Mike Foreman for agreeing with her.

Thanks also to Roger Davis, Patricia Atkins, and Diane Kokes of the Palmer Lake Historical Society, who helped us find many of the historical photos used in this book and thanks to Sharon Williams for suggesting the cemetery project to John.

Michael would also like to thank his wife, Tia M. Mayer, for her support and editing skills as well as her constant encouragement.

We also appreciate the help given to us by Madeline VanDenHoek, Amy Martin, and of course our wonderful publisher, Filter Press.

# About the Authors

Cowriting the history of Monument Cemetery is but one of John Howe's volunteer projects. He is a board member and integral part of the town's monthly newspaper, *Our Community News*. He is on the board of the Monument Sanitation District, is a former member of the Board of Trustees, and can often be seen around town wearing one of his trademark Hawaiian shirts.

*Images courtesy of Krista Bobo*

Michael Weinfeld lives in Monument with his wife, Tia M. Mayer. They moved here from Herndon, Virginia in 2018. Weinfeld worked for Associated Press Broadcast in New York City and Washington, DC for thirty-three years starting as a news reporter, writer, and radio anchor before creating the AP's first entertainment division. He has interviewed hundreds of Hollywood's biggest celebrities. Weinfeld is now one of the editors of *Our Community News*, and despite living in Colorado, he remains a lifelong Red Sox fan.

# Index

Adams, Charles, 15, 22
Anderson, Mildred, 98, 100, 102
Arms, Skip, 17
Ashworth, R. H., 87, 88
Assam, Jeanne, 17
Bailey, John, 108, 109, 110, 111
Barry, Clarrisa, 71
Beck, Dr. Richard, 100
Bennet, Hamilton, 72
Bishop, Vergal, 70, 76
Bissell, Charles, 9, 54, 85, 86, 87
Bougher, John, 95
Brown, Francis M., 12, 13
Case, Linda
   Monument historian, 8, 20, 32, 119, 123
Chandler, Alice, 53
Chandler, Moses, 52, 53, 123
Chase, T. J., 78, 79, 120
Cowger, Brad, 109, 110, 111, 112, 113
Crematory Garden, 105, 106
Crouse, Philip, 17
Curry, Bertha, 91
Davidson, Daniel, 12, 13, 14
Denver & Rio Grande Railroad, 6, 15, 45
Doyle, Mary, 36, 39

Doyle, William, 36
Doyle, William E., 36
Eckerson, Everett, 77, 78
Erickson, Tina, 84, 124
Ford, Charles, 40, 41, 42
Ford, Colonel Francis Ripley, 40, 41
Ford, Henrietta
   wife of Francis Ripley Ford, 41, 42
Foreman, Mike
   Town Manager, 124
GeoModel, Inc. 114
Griffith, Kent, 116, 117
ground-penetrating radar, 83, 114
Guire, David, 28, 30, 31
Guire, Henry, 5, 28, 29, 30, 99, 119, 123
Guire, Jake, 28
Guire, Joseph, 29
Guire, Josiah, 28
Guire, Mary Ann
   wife of Henry Guire, 28, 29, 30, 99
Hafen, LeRoy
   state historian, 22
Hagedorn, Lela, 87, 106
Haight, Susie, 109, 110, 111
Hanks, Thomas A., 36
Hassell Iron Works, 73, 74

Helton, Vilna, 67
Henry's Station, 6, 15, 52
Higbee, Catherine Anstine, 43
Higby Mercantile Company, 44
Higby, Emily Marie (Briley), 43, 46
Higby, John William, 43, 44, 46, 123
Hilleman, Ron, 99, 107, 109, 110, 111, 112
Hillen, Harry, 78, 79, 80, 119, 120
Hogan, Laura
   Town Clerk, 124
Howe, John, iii, 1, 3, 4, 55, 56, 85, 115, 116, 117, 125
Johnson, Tiffany, 17
Karn, Al
   Police Chief, 112
Kendall, Margaret Alice
   wife of Paton Wilson, 35
Lavelett, Lucille
   author, Through the Years at Monument, Colorado, 13, 14, 15, 20, 27, 33, 37, 54, 85, 87, 91, 94, 95, 96, 97, 98, 100, 103, 108, 120
Limbach, Caroline (Lindner), 14, 15, 16
Limbach, Henry, 6, 12, 14, 15, 16
Lolley's Ice Cream, 5
Martin, Amy, 112
Martin, Toni, 107, 109, 110, 112
Mayer, Tia M.
   wife of Michael Weinfeld, 4, 124, 125
McPhail, Jerry, 97, 98
McShane, Albert, 22
McShane, Catherine, 5, 18, 19, 22, 23, 29
McShane, David, 5, 13, 18, 19, 21, 22, 23, 25, 29, 32, 50
Monument Homemakers Club, 94
Monument Hotel, 27, 39, 41, 119
Monument Public Works, 23
Munson, John, 68, 69
Murray, Matthew, 16
Neilon, Barbara, 58
Newbrough, James Walter, 50, 51, 52
Olfs, Christine, 32, 33
Olfs, John, 32, 33
Palmer Lake Historical Society, 5, 48, 66, 120, 124
Plowman, Margaret, 96, 98, 100, 101, 102, 103, 105, 107, 108, 110, 111
Rathburn, Ron, 23
Routt, Eliza, 7
Routt, John
   Colorado governor, 7
Rupp, Mary K., 27
Rupp, William H., 26, 27
Russell, John, 34
Savage Sabin, Marion
   author, Palmer Lake

A Historical Narrative, 26, 27
Simpson, Fred William, 47, 48, 49, 123
Simpson, Goldie, 49, 96, 98, 108
Simpson, James, 93
Slabaugh, Mayor Luther, 103
Sonnenburg, Rick Town Manager, 113
Stewart Iron Works, 73, 74, 75
Trigg, Isabella, 24, 25, 26, 120, 123
Weinfeld, Michael, iii, 4, 85, 124, 125
Weir, James, 105
Welty, Alonzo, 54, 87
Williams, Sharon Monument town gardner, 5, 56, 124
Wilson, Paton, 34, 35, 121, 123
Works, David, 17
Works, Rachel and Stephanie, 16, 17, 18

www.ingramcontent.com/pod-product-compliance
Lightning Source LLC
Chambersburg PA
CBHW042050290426
44110CB00001B/8